ON THE ROAD TO FREEDOM: A PILGRIMAGE IN INDIA

By Neal Rosner

Mata Amritanandamayi Center
P.O. Box 613
San Ramon, CA. 94583-0613
ph: (510) 537-9417

Mata Amritanandamayi Center
P.O. Box 613
San Ramon, CA. 94583-0613
ph: (510) 537-9417

Printed in the United States of America

First printing 1987

ISBN 0-9615875-4-7

Library of Congress Catalogue Card Number

87-071831

Front cover art by Bruce Hartman. Copyright © 1987 Cassandra Press.

Table of Contents

Dedication

This book is dedicated to that Infinite Being Who shines within as the Light of Awareness and without as the Holy Mother of Bliss, Mata Amritanandamayi.

Introduction

This book has been written on the insistence of a few fellow seekers who felt that my life and experiences with some of the genuine sages of India over the past 20 years would be interesting and useful to other aspirants on the spiritual path. On hearing their request I was immediately put in mind of the words of one of these saints who told me that only a Realized Soul should write a book on spirituality. If an ignorant person (ignorant in the sense of absence of Supreme Knowledge or Enlightenment) should do so, he will only fall into the trap of egoism and have a spiritual fall. I told the same to these well-wishers who, however, persisted in their request. At last I told them that if my Spiritual Master, Mata Amritanandamayi, should tell me to write the book, then only would I do it, knowing that Her Grace would protect and guide me. After these friends had approached and spoken to Her, She told me that I should write the book as a service to other aspirants.

Though this book takes the form of an autobiography, its sole purpose is to bring out the greatness and methods of teaching of some present day sages of India. If one feels inspired to seek their holy company and get the wonderful fruits thereof after reading it, then it has more than fulfilled its purpose. As the ancient sage Narada has said in the *Narada Bhakti Sutras* or Aphorisms on Devotion,

"Rare is the company of the great sages; inaccessible, but unfailing it is, to be gained by the Lord's Grace alone."

It is my conviction that although it is true that there have always been and always will be charlatans in the guise of saints, perhaps more today than in the past, still if one is sincere and intense in one's quest for the Real, one will surely find a real saint or sage to guide and protect one on the spiritual path which has been likened to the razor's edge in its difficulty to tread without feeling. As long as mankind exists on this earth, there will be such Realized Souls to guide them and quench their thirst for real spiritual experience and peace of mind. One need not think that only those who are well known are great. Indeed, most of the real saints are relatively unknown to the outside world. Blessed indeed are the sages who are blissful themselves and make others blissful as well.

Chapter 1

BEGINNINGS: Chicago to India

"I have read that many people on the spiritual path get what may be called a glimpse of Cosmic Consciousness. Would you please explain to me what, exactly, such an experience is like?" I asked.

Ratnamji, a little known but great mystic of India, unhesitatingly replied with a slightly mischievous smile on his beaming face. "When, on a dark night there is suddenly a flash of lightning, if you are on a hill like this, all the surrounding area, which had been quite invisible just a moment ago, becomes clear and lit up for just a few seconds. The very next moment, however, all is dark again."

As soon as he finished his sentence, a lightning bolt streaked across the sky. The entire area for miles around us became illumined for a second and then all was dark. Though the sky was cloudy, there had been no lightning until then. I was quite thrilled to see his example immediately and dramatically demonstrated by Mother Nature Herself, and I wondered who was this that Nature waits upon. I did not ask anything else. In a daze, I went back to my room and laid down to sleep wondering if I would be able to meet that wonderful man again.

I could not, however, fall asleep. I could hardly believe my good luck in having come into the presence of a real sage without even having made a search. Was I dreaming? How did I come to this holy place half way around the world? My mind flashed back to the incidents of the past which had eventually led to my leaving America and coming to India. It had started with the death of my father some seven years ago.

"Oh, my God! Neal, come quickly! There's something wrong with Daddy!"

When I came running into my parents bedroom, I found my father unconscious with a gurgling sound emitting from his throat. Calmly but quickly I laid him flat on the bed and started to massage his heart, occasionally pressing it vigorously as I had seen on a TV program about people suffering from heart failure. He did not seem to respond at all so I immediately called the family doctor and the police. My mother and sister were hysterical; I led them from the room and waited for the police. Help soon arrived but my father was beyond all reviving—heart failure at the age of 44. He was a successful businessman on his way to becoming a millionaire. He had never been seriously ill but was unexpectedly snatched away by death.

Relatives began to arrive and tried to comfort my mother and sister, but to little avail. Then they turned to me, the youngest in the family. I was 12 at the time. I felt quite calm and detached without the slightest inclination to cry. Perhaps this shocked my relatives. I went for a walk and thought over the meaning of what had happened. Where had my father gone? His body was lying in the bedroom and would soon be interred. I would never see him again. I felt a slight feeling of emptiness, but nothing more than that. More than anything, I felt out of place; all were crying but I was my usual self. Throughout the funeral I tried my utmost to cry, feeling somewhat guilty that everyone was weeping except me,but to no avail. Tears simply would not come. It was not that I did not love my father, but somehow the element of attachment was absent.

Soon after my father's death, the inevitable desires of youth started to sprout in my mind. I came alive, as it were, to the world around me. Although I was attending school, my only thought was how to go out and enjoy the world. My mother was no obstruction to that as she hesitated to control me, thinking that I had suffered a great loss with the death of my father. Perhaps she felt that enforced discipline would be an additional source of suffering to me, or maybe she simply lacked the stern nature of a father. Had she found a way to control me at that impressionable stage of my life, my later spiritual life might have been much smoother than it was. Owing to my selfishness and arrogance and her lenient nature, I was allowed to grow like wild grass.

Freedom was my middle name. I did not know at that

time that, though similar in appearance, freedom and anarchy are poles apart. True freedom is born out of intense inner discipline and is characterized by an internal calm unaffected by the inevitable ups and downs of life. Anarchy, on the other hand, is to dance to the tune of the mind's whims and moods without thought of the consequences. Far from enjoying the bliss and peace of freedom, the anarchist is always restless, being a slave of his impulses and buffeted here and there by the alternating waves of pleasure and pain that make up life. Without systematically disciplining one's mind, true freedom is out of the question. At that time, of course, I neither knew nor cared about the difference between the two.

When I graduated from high school, my mother asked me what I would like as a graduation present. I told her that I would like very much to go to Europe for the summer before deciding on my future course of education. She agreed and soon I was touring Europe alone. Full of anticipation, I went from place to place and visited countless famous historical monuments and works of art such as the Eiffel Tower, Westminster Abbey and Leonardo de Vinci's sculptures. Somehow, they all seemed the same—simply brick, cement, wood, or iron arranged in different ways. Nothing brought any response from me. The expected thrilling tour turned out to be a bore.

I thought perhaps there was something wrong with me. How was it possible that millions of tourists were being thrilled by these sights while I remained unmoved? Though only 17 at the time, I started to question myself seriously about the purpose of my life. I found no satisfactory answer. Enjoyment and pleasure seemed to be the immediate goals of my life but, I had already experienced my first disillusionment with this tour. Perhaps future pleasure seeking would be more profitable, or was pleasure only a projection of my mind? What was a source of so much happiness to so many left me unmoved. I returned to America, disappointed and somewhat puzzled, yet determined to find that which would make me happy

Upon my return from Europe, my elder brother Earl invited me to visit him in Ann Arbor, Michigan where he was studying for his master of arts degree. Making the journey from Chicago by car, I arrived around supper time. I was surprised to find that my brother had become a vegetarian. He was noticeably trimmer, healthier, and calmer than when I had last seen him. I asked him what had made him change his eating habits.

"Six months ago I began learning and practicing hatha yoga. I found a teacher here in Ann Arbor who spent several years in India studying yoga under a master. She is quite an unusual person. I want you to meet her. She explained to me that food has a dual nature, subtle and gross. The gross part makes up the body, and the subtle essence affects the nature of the mind. The subtle component of vegetarian food is better for health and gradually gives a more gentle nature to the mind, which in turn makes it easier to meditate. By meditation one can experience the bliss of Self-Realization, a bliss incomparable with worldly pleasure. To know through direct intuitive experience that one is not the physical body or restless mind but rather an imperishable infinite mass of Pure Existence and Bliss is Self-Realization or the knowledge of one's True Nature. There have been many who have achieved that state and they have told that the real goal of life lies in that Experience. We can go to see her tomorrow."

India, yoga, meditation...a flicker of light flashed in my, until then, dead heart. I was eager and at the same time frightened at the prospect of meeting a "yogini." I expected that she would be something out of the fourth dimension. In the morning, my brother took me to his yoga teacher's house. What a surprise; she was a human being after all! Barbara was a middle-aged woman, lively, sweet, and natural. I felt a relief; I had expected to see a grave figure levitating four feet off the ground while standing on her head! We became friends immediately. She gave me a copy of the *Bhagavad Gita,* a well known work on yoga and asked me to read it. After eating lunch with her and talking about some ordinary matters, we returned to Earl's house. A brief meeting, but perhaps the most momentous one of my life. Little did I realize at the time that the seed of spirituality had been sown and would soon sprout and grow into the spreading tree of deep inner peace.

In the evening I took up the copy of the *Bhagavad Gita.*

The *Bhagavad Gita* is perhaps the most revered of all Hindu scriptures and contains the essence of all of them. It is part of a much larger work, the *Mahabharata*, and contains the philosophy of the science of Self Knowledge as taught by Sri Krishna, an Incarnation of God, to His devotee Arjuna while on a battlefield. It has been widely acclaimed by many of the most renowned scholars the world over as containing the highest wisdom attainable by man. I could not even pronounce the title but, hoping for the best, I commenced reading.

As I read, every word caused a thrill to go through my heart. I felt as if I were Arjuna and Sri Krishna was talking directly to me. All the questions which had been weighing on my mind were being answered, and even questions which had not formed themselves became clear and doubts dispelled. Until reading the *Bhagavad Gita*, I never knew what the word "wisdom" meant. The nature of the mind and the goal of life were revealed in unambiguous language. Obviously, or so it seemed to me, the purpose of life was not to seek and enjoy sensual pleasures endlessly until death. Rather it was to understand the mind clearly, purify it, and go beyond it to experience Reality where quiet Bliss alone reigns supreme. For the first time since I was a little boy, I cried. These tears were not born out of sorrow or selfishness but out of joy. I did not sleep that night, my thirst was so great to complete the book. Now and then my brother came in to see what was the matter. What could I answer? I had entered another world, as it were, that night.

The next day I decided to adopt a vegetarian diet. Naive as I was, I thought that this would be enough to achieve Self-Realization! I was expecting to achieve the highest state of samadhi (absorption into the Supreme Reality) in a matter of a few days! I spent several days with my brother and then returned to Chicago, happy to have found some direction in my life.

I decided that I did not want to go directly into college. It seemed to me that the ultimate purpose of such institutionalized education was to enable one to make money, which in turn would make it possible to enjoy the so-called pleasures of life. I felt that a very simple life that did not require much money would be enough for me so a modest job would do.   Why should I spend four or six years of my life in a college?

This decision, of course, was disappointing to my mother. She had expected me to lead a more normal life of going to college, but she agreed to my proposal.   Hoping that I would change my mind later, she allowed me to have my own way. Selling my telescope, coin collection, car, and other possessions which a typical upper middle class American teenager would have, I decided to go to the west coast and find a quiet place in the countryside where I could eat vegetarian food and meditate! Besides, my sensuous appetites were not as yet completely satisfied. Although I had read the *Bhagavad Gita,* I had not yet understood that unless the senses are controlled the mind would never become calm. Without a calm mind, successful meditation and the resultant Realization of the Self would be impossible. As with any other science, the science of yoga must be followed according to the rules and procedures laid down, if one wishes to get the desired results. I erroneously thought that Self-Realization, being the enjoyment of Supreme Bliss, could be attained through a little haphazard effort coupled with good luck just as the pleasures and enjoyments of the world are.

In the company of a few friends, I drove my sister's car to Berkeley, California in the autumn of 1967. Vegetarianism was not popular in America in those days, and finding that kind of food while traveling presented a real difficulty. How long could one live on cheese sandwiches? I thought perhaps spiritual life was not for me, but the shame of having to admit defeat so soon after starting prevented me from giving up. On reaching Berkeley, I set myself to the task of finding the ideal house in just the right kind of surroundings. This was not as easy as I had thought it would be. After searching for many days and driving many miles in all directions around Berkeley, a sense of defeat and resignation took hold of me. At that very moment, without even having to search any further, an ideal house caught my attention and I took it for rent. It was large enough to accommodate all of us and more also. I wrote to my brother and sister, and they decided to move to California and soon joined me.

One of the main interests of my life became the attainment of Self-Realization but, to be perfectly honest, even more than that was the desire to live with a woman. This is quite a normal desire for any teenage American boy but living at home with my mother had made it difficult. This undoubtedly was one of my reasons for leaving Chicago and going to California, which was at that time the haven of such people as myself. After I settled down in the new house, my thoughts centered around the achievement of my immediate goal. Being somewhat reserved by nature, I decided that if I were to get a suitable companion, it would have to be in the same way that I found the present house—that is, by Providence. So I made no effort to find a girlfriend. Strange as it may seem, the very next day a girl appeared at my door. She was looking for me! She had heard of me in Chicago, and had come to California searching for me. Whether she was telling the truth or not I did not know, nor did I care to know as my wish was resolved of its own accord.

The impact of this experience on my mind was such that I began to believe earnestly that whatever was really necessary for me would be provided. In fact, up to the present time, I have experienced the truth of this countless times. Of course, what is needed will naturally differ according to time and place and may be painful as well as pleasant. However, if one is patient and keeps his goal as the Realization of God, one will find the circumstances forming themselves for one's spiritual progress. At that time, a girlfriend was what I needed. Later, the company of sages was essential. Still later, sickness and suffering became necessary. In fact, whatever is happening at the present moment is for the best, in the eyes of spiritual aspirants, and is being provided at the right time in a most mysterious way.

After Earl arrived, he gave me a new book to read. It was the life and teachings of a great sage of India, Sri Ramana Maharshi. Ramana, when a boy of 16 years, was suddenly overcome with the fear of death. There was nothing wrong with his health, nor was there any reason that such a fear should arise at that time. Still, he felt that he would die and that he must solve the problem then and there. He lay down and simulated death. Then he thought to himself, "Now the body is dead, but I still feel the sense of 'I' shining within. I am therefore the deathless Spirit and not the inert body." This did not come to him as a logical conclusion, but rather as a flash of intuition and direct experience. This was not a mere glimpse of Reality to be covered over soon after by the darkness of ignorance. From that moment, the awareness of himself as pure Spirit beyond death remained intact until his departure from the body some 53 years later in 1950. Just before his death, Ramana assured his devotees that he would continue to be with them and guide them in spite of the death of the physical body. Having attained Realization through a spontaneous act of inwardly enquiring, "Who am I?" eliminating the body and mind as his real Being, and clearly experiencing himself to be Pure Awareness transcending all, he became free of all desire and fear, even the fear of death, and remained established in perfect peace. Ramana lived near a holy mountain, Arunachala, in the southern part of India, radiating spiritual light and peace. He became a living example of the ideal conduct of a Self-Realized sage in daily life. As the means to attaining that State, he advocated either the continuous guidance of and surrender to an Enlightened Being or independently pursuing the path of self-inquiry. By adopting either approach, one will acquire the necessary serenity and concentration to experience the Truth within.

His teaching and life had great appeal for me, and I decided to practice both methods. Self-inquiry took the form of sitting quietly repeating "I, I, I..." to myself while trying to fix my attention on the meaning of the word, the thing within me which shines as "I." In my day-to-day life I tried to practice surrender to Ramana, whom I took as my Master, by accepting the circumstances in which I found myself without reacting either positively to the pleasant or negatively to the painful. My brother taught me some hatha yogic postures for improving my health and purifying my nervous system. All this helped give some discipline to my otherwise loose life. At that time I thought I would get married and lead a mixture of spiritual and worldly life, or a spiritualized worldly life. However, it was to be otherwise.

One day a letter came for Earl from his yoga teacher in Michigan. It said, "I am very glad to hear that Neal is practicing the postures as taught by you. He is still young. Why does he not become a monk and dedicate himself completely to the attainment of the Self?" He showed me the letter. After reading it I felt like a person who is suddenly given a bitter herb while eating sweet pudding. I was quite happy with my girlfriend and my meditation practice, and had no intention of giving up either. I dismissed the matter from my mind and went about my usual routine.

A few days later, while meditating, my concentration suddenly became intense and my dispersed mind resolved itself into a single point. The mind, like a small light, became extinguished at which moment infinite Light, Perfect Bliss, and all-pervading Oneness alone remained. All trace of individuality and objectivity was lost. Then, like a descending elevator, my mind came back into existence and became aware of the body and the world, but the next moment again merged into the Light. This repeated itself three or four times, after which I was weeping and sobbing like a small baby at the thought of that tremendous Peace and Vastness. The revelation that I would once again merge into that Supreme Light forever, after undergoing many painful lessons in life, appeared as a certainty from within.

I felt that Ramana was in some inexplicable way responsible for this sublime experience, for had I not mentally surrendered my life to him? He had assured his devotees that he would be with them even after the death of his body, and so he must surely be with me as well. However, I was under a grand illusion that having such a wonderful experience after only a few days of meditation meant that if I continued to meditate I would get the same experience again and again until it became permanent, all within a few weeks at the most! Needless to say, this was not the case, although the memory as well as the taste of that Bliss has remained ever after. Somehow a glimpse of the Goal was vouchsafed, and now it was for me to walk the steep path leading to It.

From that time onwards a gradual transformation of my mind started to take place. I felt a very subtle, light intoxi-

cation after doing yoga. It was not just physical invigora-
tion but rather a feeling of blissful detachment from the body
and the world. I also found that keeping intimate company
with the fair sex caused that bliss to vanish almost totally
until I would do the yogic exercises again. Though the animal pleasures of sex were very attractive, they seemed
very crude indeed compared to the subtle spiritual bliss. I
could not however simply give up sex, nor was I willing to
go on losing my newly found treasure of spiritual experience. I therefore decided to avoid the company of my
girlfriend as much as possible and so, after yoga in the
morning, I would take the car and go up into the hills behind
Berkeley. I read spiritual books, meditated and gazed upon
the hills and valleys until sunset. The very thought of having to return to my girlfriend after sunset used to depress
me, and with great reluctance I would return to the house.
This routine went on for some days but did not seem to
solve the problem. My girlfriend started to suspect that I
was seeing another girl during the day, which made her
determined to possess me even more during the night.

This situation made me perceive the relationship between a man and a woman as one based primarily on self-
interest. If she really loved me as she said she did, would
she not try to make me happy instead of miserable? I had
explained my spiritual experiences to her and my reasons
for going to the mountains during the daytime and also the
effect of sexual intimacy on my inner bliss. In fact, with the
trust of an innocent child I did not hide anything from her,
but she could only think of her own pleasure. I asked her
one day, "If I should shave my head and beard, would you
still love me? Or if I could no longer have sex with you,
would you still love me?" A shocked expression came
over her face, but she did not give a reply to my question.
From this I came to understand that what we were calling
love was nothing but a mutual satisfying of selfish desires,
physical and mental. For the most part, it was based only
on the physical attraction which we felt for each other and
maybe a slight mental affinity. This so-called love was very
shallow and any disagreement could bring it tumbling
down.

I did not know at that time of the self-effacing Divine

love of great saints for suffering humanity, but I did know that such a superficial love was of little value to me. I wondered how I could extricate myself from the present situation without hurting her already troubled mind. Moreover, the words of my brother's yoga teacher, "Become a monk, become a monk,"started to haunt me, and I began to feel that was what I should do. But how?

At this time Barbara, Earl's yoga teacher, moved to Kathmandu, Nepal with her husband who had been transferred there in government service. My brother asked me if I would like to accompany him and his wife and baby to Nepal as he was eager to see Barbara as well as to see India. He said that on the way I could enter a Zen Buddhist monastery and become a Zen monk if it suited me. I took this as my golden opportunity to escape from my predicament and immediately agreed to accompany him. I made some temporary financial arrangement for my girlfriend. I promised to write to her and, if possible, even send for her. I wanted our separation to be as painless for her as possible. I did not even think of the absurdity of what I was proposing although she did. "What will I do in a monastery even if I should come?" she asked, a bit angry at my apparent insincerity. It was my turn to have no answer.

At last the day of departure arrived and after a brief goodby at the dock, I bid farewell to my mother, girlfriend, and my few friends who had come to see us off. When at last the ship rolled away from the dock, I heaved a deep sigh of relief. I was giving up all that was familiar to me, yet somehow, I felt quite indifferent to it all. I recalled the same feeling of detachment at the time of my father's death. Like the bow of the ship breaking through the waves, my life was moving forward and I wondered what lay ahead of me, what lay ahead of me?

As the ship pulled out of San Francisco Bay, I climbed to the upper deck and sat down. Though only 18 at the time, I felt as if I had passed through a long married life and was now like a man who had somehow climbed out of a deep abyss. My faith in Ramana had obviously not been misplaced. I felt that he had somehow gotten me out of a very difficult situation. As I sat there viewing the deck below, I suddenly felt as if something very gently pressed the top of my head and a great peace began to flow within my mind. The movements of the mind became stilled and, as I looked down, I could see men and women talking with each other on the deck. It became, for lack of a better word, "revealed" to me that the attraction between the sexes was the most powerful urge in nature responsible for much of mankind's ceaseless activity. This may seem a very elementary realization, and I admit that it is, but at that moment it was truly a new revelation to me.

At that moment I knew that I would not follow the same path as the ordinary man, the path of pleasure, but that I would strive to attain the infinite bliss of the Self or die in the attempt. Although I knew nothing of orthodox monasticism or even that celibacy is prescribed as an essential discipline for attaining Enlightenment, somehow I felt the need for a chaste life dedicated to a sublime goal. I had neither read nor been told that the sexual urge needed to be controlled and sublimated. I came to that conclusion through my own experience.

Earl and I had decided to take a ship rather than a plane because we were eager to continue our practice of yoga punctually without any break. We were regularly doing the postures for one hour in the morning and one hour in the evening. Also, there was some time devoted to meditation and the study of spiritual books. We were in no hurry to reach Japan, and the leisurely speed of boat travel suited our life style. While all were still sleeping, I would rise at 4:30 in the morning, have a shower and do yoga and meditation on the deck. The pure air, the silence of the vast sea, and the grandeur of the daily drama of the rising sun soothed my mind. But the restlessness to achieve Spiritual Realization caused a continuous feeling of burning in my heart.

Somehow a childlike faith in a great sage had sprouted in my heart. I had never in my life thought of God except on one or two occasions when, as a child, I could find no other way to get a thing I badly wanted and so I prayed to Him, as an experiment. What was my wonder when I got my beloved wish granted! My parents were both agnostics and had sent me to Sunday school probably for the simple reason that the rest of the children in the community were going and not out of any belief or fear of God. God only seemed to be a word to be used in conjunction with other words like "God forbid", "only God knows," and "God damn it!"

Even at this point I never thought of God, the Universal Being, as the one guiding my new life, but rather Ramana, who had promised to guide his devotees which now included me! I never rationalized how that could be possible. How could one man control another's life circumstances? Especially a man who had lived 12,000 miles away and had died 18 years ago. Well, Ramana had realized the Self and as such, he was and is not different from the Supreme who has no birth and death. Taking this as a gospel truth, I experienced it every moment from that time onwards.

My personality was undergoing a deep change at a very fast rate. While talking to others on the boat, I would listen to their problems with a new feeling of sympathy. I started to see that everyone, however happy, was still in search of more and better happiness. Satisfaction of one desire only made way for another. People did not seem to know or care that there was anything beyond mundane happiness. Their only concern seemed to be with money, sex, fame, and health. In the pursuit of these things, they were getting only a penny of pleasure for a pound of sweat. Before one realized it, old age and death would take one away.

A heaviness of heart came over me as I thought: Is this all there is to the average man's life? Birth, seeking for pleasure, and then death? I had enjoyed a glimpse of a happiness which lies beyond the pale of the senses and mind. I was pursuing the spiritual path, but what about the others? As I could not find any satisfactory answer to my doubts, I began to see man's life and problems from a sympathetic viewpoint, not desiring anything from anyone but giving whatever I could. It seemed to me that selfishness blinded one to everything except one's own little circumscribed world, like the proverbial frog in the well.

One day while browsing in the ship's library, I came across a book written by Swami Sivananda of Rishikesh, a village at the foot of the Himalayas. Apparently his disciple, Swami Chidananda, had taken this same ship at some other time and had donated the book to the library. It touched on all aspects of spiritual life. While reading it, I came across the statement that whoever one may be, if one wants to attain Self-Realization, the company of a living Master is essential. I started to ponder what to do. Was Ramana not enough? At night after everyone had gone to sleep, I went up on the ship's deck with an aching heart.

For the first time in my life I wept from the bottom of my heart, crying out into the dark night," O Ramana! What am I to do? Without a Master, how is it possible to reach the Goal? Who will show me the way and teach me how to lead a spiritual life? Is it possible that there exists another as great as you? I will accept no one less than you. Will you not show me the way?" I wept and wept like a small child. I had never experienced such sorrow or known what bliss there could be in crying one's heart out to the Supreme. I came to see in the coming months that my prayer had, indeed, been heard.

The boat stopped at Hawaii, and we went sightseeing for the day. We drove a rented car around the island and came to a beautiful beach with turquoise water, blue sky, and sharp jagged cliffs receding from the sea. The scenery was indeed enchanting, but my mind was somewhere else. I could relish nothing, somewhat like a man sorrowing for his beloved, absent-minded and unable to partake in anything wholeheartedly. Earl and his wife were enjoying the place immensely, and to avoid making them feel uneasy on my account, I also made a show of interest and pleasure.

After a few more days at sea, we reached Japan. As we disembarking at Yokohama, Earl decided that we should take a train to Kyoto, the City of Temples. Within a few hours, we arrived at the place that was to be my new home for the next four months.

After we had settled down at a comfortable inn, Earl felt that the first thing to be done was to search for Gary Snyder, a well-known American poet whom we knew to be living in Kyoto. He had visited Ramana Maharshi's Ashram in India and had contributed some poems to the ashram's quarterly journal. As devotees of Ramana, we thought that we could approach him for advice regarding a place to stay and sights to see. After three or four hours, we had all but given up hope of finding his residence when an English-speaking gentleman pointed it out to us.

Gary was very friendly and hospitable. He invited us in and asked his wife to prepare tea for all of us. He told us that he had lived as a Zen monk in a monastery for eight years and that afterwards he decided to get married. He married a Japanese girl and they had recently had a small baby. He was engaged in translating some of the Buddhist scriptures into English as well as writing poetry. In fact, he was planning to return to America to live and start a spiritual community. He would have gladly leased out his house to us on his departure for America, but he had already promised it to someone else. He assured us that he would find us a suitable place the next day and would meet us at our inn.

Gary then turned towards me and asked me about my plans. I told him that I desired to become a monk, perhaps a Zen monk, but I was not sure. I asked him if there was any place where I could get a taste of that kind of life. He seemed to be very happy to hear about my aspiration and said that he would show me such a place after we were settled. I felt very peaceful and at ease in his presence and thought that he surely must have achieved a good level of spirituality through his Zen training. I hoped that he would give me some guidance along the spiritual path, and I was not disappointed. When we left, he showed us to the door. In all oriental countries, one takes off one's shoes before entering the house. We had left our shoes at the door. Gary took a glance at them. One pair was neatly placed, while the others were haphazardly strewn about. He waited to see whose shoes belonged to whom. On seeing me put on the first pair he smiled and said, "I can tell the mind of a man by a simple thing like this. One who is interested in meditation should always be mindful and lead an orderly and concentrated life. Only then will it be possible to get one-pointedness in meditation."

I was very happy to hear such practical advice, and even today I think of Gary when I remove my shoes before entering a place. This quality of taking to heart appropriate advice and putting it into practice until it's fruit is realized began at that moment. Though the advice was minor, its implications were vast. Not only placing the shoes, but every action should be done with concentration and care. I decided to try my utmost to follow his advice.

The next morning, Gary came to our inn and after breakfast we set out in search of a house. I felt the happiness of one who had found a long lost friend. For some inexplicable reason I began to feel bound to Gary in a spiritual way. It was a new experience, which was to be repeated many times in the future with other people

Gary took us to a number of houses. In Japan a stranger does not approach anyone directly concerning an important matter. One must go through a mediator. Though a bit troublesome, it assures both parties that the other is dependable, in other words, prevention is better than cure. This sound practice holds true throughout the orient. At last we found a very comfortable two-story house for a reasonable rent. We settled in within the next few days.

One evening Gary invited us to go with him to a nearby Zen temple. He told me that a small meditation center attached to the temple was run and supervised by a Japanese Zen Master. Lay people were allowed to sit there for meditation three or four nights a week under the supervision of the Roshi, or Master, and his assistant. He asked if I would like to try meditating there. Eagerly I replied in the affirmative.

We arrived around 5:30 p.m. The center was a small compound attached to the outside wall of the main Zen temple. Inside there was a very pleasant small Japanese garden, a library and sitting room, accommodation for the Roshi, and a meditation hall, or zendo. After exchanging a few words with the Roshi, Gary ushered Earl and me into the Zendo, and the three of us took our seats on the raised platform. I did not know what to expect, so I observed what the other 20 people were doing. A gong was rung and they sat up erect on their cushions. I sat in the half-lotus posture and tried to meditate on the "I" within. I could see the Roshi's assistant slowly pacing up and down the hall with a flat stick in his hand, and I wondered what it was used for. My question was soon answered. He came over to the man next to me and lightly tapped him on the shoulder with the stick. After saluting each other with joined palms oriental style, the man next to me bent over and received two sharp whacks on his back with the stick. I jumped with fright!

Fearing the whack, I could no longer concentrate. My mind was on the man with the stick! After half an hour, my legs became numb and my back started to bend. I dared not move lest I get whacked. I thought my legs would fall off or, at least, would never come back to life again! The assistant continued to slowly pace the hall. Then to my great chagrin, he stopped before me and tapped me on the shoulder with the stick. Sweating profusely, I saluted him and bent over and WHACK. It was over before I knew what had happened. There was a burning sensation but no pain. On the other hand, I felt invigorated immediately afterwards and sat up straight. My legs however continued to feel wooden.

After 40 minutes, the gong was rung. Rising from their cushions, the meditators filed out of the zendo and walked briskly and silently around it for five minutes, trying to continue their meditation. Then they returned to the zendo and continued their meditation. This activity was repeated one more time. Then some monks chanted the Prajnaparamita Sutra in resounding tones and all prostrated themselves. Afterwards, they went to the sitting room to be with the Roshi for a few minutes and to drink some tea. The Roshi, though nearly 60 years old, radiated a childlike innocence. I asked him how he had attained such a state of happiness.

"I became a monk at the age of eight. I was convinced of the truth of the Buddha's teachings and applied myself fully to the task of attaining Enlightenment. When World War II broke out, even monks were drafted into military service but there were two or three who were exempted upon the grounds of their dedication to monastic life. I was one of them. I have worked so hard to achieve my present happy state that I used to feel as if my bones would break. If you wish the same for yourself, you too must be ready to break your bones."

After drinking tea, we returned to the house. Gary went his own way after telling us that we could sit in the zendo four nights a week at the same hours. On the way home, I felt very humiliated, not painfully, but refreshingly so. Subconsciously I had thought very highly of myself, but my pride and arrogance had received a blow at the hands of the assistant's stick. The words of the Roshi echoed in my ears. I decided that, come what may, I would return to the zendo the next sitting day and "break my bones."

After two days Earl and I returned to the meditation center. I directly entered the zendo and found a place to sit. The summer heat was oppressive and the mosquitos were having a feast. There was not even a slight breeze inside the zendo. Well, I had come to break my bones, had I not I? The sitting started with the ringing of the gong. I had just started to meditate when my mind became deeply concentrated. Thoughts decreased and the feeling "I am" clearly manifested itself as a kind of subtle illumination or current of light within. I felt quite clearly that I was neither the body nor the mind but only that current of light. I was elated. Even at the end of the sitting this experience persisted. When Earl and I left the zendo at the end of the meditation session, I almost collided with an oncoming bus. I found it quite impossible to give my attention to outside things and did not really care what would happen as a consequence. Fortunately, Earl caught me by the arm and asked what was the matter. I thought that he may not believe me or that there may be some hint of pride in my voice. After thinking it over, I carefully replied:

"While meditating in there I suddenly felt as if I am 'I' only and not the body. In fact, the body seemed to be quite a foreign object, different from myself. Even now that feeling is persisting. Also, my mind feels as if it has been washed clean with cool water and has a calm and pure sensation. I am only now starting to understand a little of the meaning of Ramana's teachings."

Earl seemed to be buried in his own thoughts, and we reached the house without talking any more. For about half an hour, that feeling of illumination persisted; then it gradually disappeared. I was naturally eager to regain that state and looked forward to returning to the zendo. Each time I returned to meditate in the Zendo, I had the same experience of clarity and cool, pure light. The heat, mosquitos, and leg pains only made me cling more intensely to my inner calm. After each session, I felt that my mind had taken a cool shower, and though the summer heat was unbearable, I was under the impression that the weather was quite pleasant. This experience of inner light persisted for some time after meditation and then, as before, faded away.

One day Gary invited us to his house for a picnic. On reaching there, we found about eight or ten other foreigners who were apparently some of his friends. We all went to a hill near the house and sat in a circle with Gary in the center. He then began to sing:

"Hari Krishna Hari Krishna Krishna Krishna Hari Hari Hari Rama Hari Rama Rama Rama Hari Hari."

He was singing with his whole heart, and it seemed as if he would cry. I felt very moved and was curious to know what it was that he was singing. After he finished, we all sat in silence for some time. Then I asked him about the song.

"A friend of mind who spent some time in India taught me this song. It is composed of the different Names of God. In India the Supreme Reality goes by different names. Here we may call It by the name of Buddha Nature, but there people call It Krishna, Rama, or Hari. Singing the Divine Name gives a unique bliss. One should try to merge into and become one with That while singing."

After hearing this, my interest in going to India was reawakened. Though I was no doubt getting some spiritual peace of mind due to my meditation in the zendo, the feeling that I did not belong in Japan always nagged at the back of my mind. The Buddhist culture seemed foreign to me. I did not think that I could ever consider it to be my own. We had spent four months in Japan and Earl also was anxious to continue on to India. We booked our tickets on the first boat for Bangkok, and after taking leave of Gary and his family, we were on our way.

We stopped in Manila, Hong Kong, and a few other places before reaching Bangkok. In Bangkok we found a cheap room and thought to do some sightseeing. While Earl and his wife went out to make some inquiries about places of interest, I decided to do my yoga practice. I had just finished and was sitting in the lotus posture about to meditate when there was a knock on the door. A female voice asked if she may come in. When I said yes, the door opened and in walked an attractive but very scantily dressed lady. I did not at first understand what she wanted as she was speaking in Thai language and thought that she was a member of the hotel staff. Finally, by observing her gestures it struck me that she must be a prostitute and was looking for business. I had never seen a prostitute before, or at least I had never recognized one. For a moment I felt a slight temptation. Then seeing myself sitting in the lotus position, I gained strength and said to her, "I am doing yoga. Can you not see that?" She, of course, could not understand what I was saying, nor had she probably ever seen anyone doing yoga before. She kept asking me if I wanted her to stay, and I kept saying "yoga, yoga" until she finally got impatient and went out in a huff. Well, I had somehow saved myself from a fall but felt quite miserable at my lack of mental strength to simply say "get out" outright.

Sightseeing in Thailand consisted of seeing one Buddhist temple after another. This only made me more restless to reach India, the land where Buddhism took its birth. Within a few days, we boarded a plane and reached the blessed land of the sages. While sitting in the Calcutta airport waiting for the connecting plane to Nepal, I was hardly aware of the fact of being in an airport. Every inch of land, every tree, and every person seemed to be full of holiness. I thought again and again that this is the holy land where Lord Krishna had been born and taught the Bhagavad Gita to Arjuna, where Buddha took his birth and spread the gospel of Enlightenment, and where Ramana had attained Self-Knowledge. Every bearded man appeared to me to be a saint. You could say that I was credulous, but even now after living in India for 18 years, I still feel it to be the holiest place on earth. My happiness at having arrived in India could not be expressed, but no sooner had we arrived than we were on our way to Nepal.

Upon arriving in Kathmandu we proceeded to Barbara's house. She had been my brother's yoga teacher in America and had invited us to visit with her on our way to India. She had already been the instrumental cause for many important changes in my life by giving me the *Bhagavad Gita* to read and by suggesting that I become a monk. I wondered what I might learn from her now. She and her husband had been given a beautiful and spacious three story house by the government of Nepal to stay in. It was very near to the Indian Embassy and only a few minutes walk from the rice fields. On a clear day, the snow-capped Himalayas could be seen in the distance. She had converted the upper floor of the house into a studio for practicing and teaching yoga. It was airy, with plenty of light and beautiful views all round. I was given a separate room.

Barbara had just returned to Nepal after making a trip to India. She had traveled to the southern part of India in order to visit Ramana Maharshi's ashram. She was bubbling with joy and told me that she could clearly feel Ramana's presence there. She said that the spiritual peace there was so palpable one could almost cut it with a knife. This was not the peace of a graveyard but the radiant peace surrounding a Self-Realized sage. The holy hill Arunachala seemed to be alive to Barbara and she had walked on it and around it many times experiencing a deep concentration of mind. She also told me there was a disciple of Ramana's in the ashram, Ratnamji by name, who was the real life of the ashram. In fact, she was of the opinion that without him, the ashram, though an abode of peace, would be devoid of life. Ratnamji had come to Ramana in 1942 at the young age of 20 and had become Ramana's personal attendant until 1950 when Ramana left his body. Ratnamji had then traveled all over India, keeping in close contact with some of the greatest sages in the country and serving many of them. He had devoted 30 years to intense spiritual austerity and study. He had a visible glow about him, a vast knowledge of scriptures and, above everything else, a power in his words which would raise the listener to sublime heights of understanding and experience. She told me that I should not miss meeting him.

This, of course, was more than I could bear. I was already restless to reach the ashram, and hearing these words only made my longing increase. My whole mind became possessed with the desire to pack up and run to Ramana's holy presence. Earl wanted to do some sightseeing and even proposed that we spend some time in the Himalayas. As for myself, my eyes were always fixed on the ground trying to hold on to my meditation day and night. I told him that the Himalayas would be there forever but that we would not; spiritual realization must be achieved at once. He was taken aback at my statement. I told him that I would prefer to go to India and reach Ramana's ashram as soon as possible.

With a mixture of hurt feelings and some anger, Earl told me that I could do as I liked, that I need not go along with him. Until then, he had been my guide, always concerned about my happiness and well-being. He had arranged our journey and had taken all the responsibility to see that our lives ran smoothly. It was only natural that he should feel hurt at my sudden show of independence, but what could I do? I felt like an iron filing being drawn by a strong magnet away from everything except itself. I told him this and went to buy a ticket back to India.

The next day saw me at the airport with Earl, Barbara, and her husband to see me off after staying in Nepal for only a few days. I felt a bit unsure of myself. I was striking out on my own at the age of 19. I was thousands of miles away from my own country and about to plunge headlong into a new culture about which I knew nothing. I had no plan for the future except that I must somehow reach Ramana's ashram and attain Realization of the Self. There was really no question of arguing with the inner call to leave everyone and everything. It was as clear as the sun in mid-heavens, but the uncertainty of the future frightened me a bit.

After leaving Nepal and arriving once again in Calcutta, I caught the first plane to Madras in southern India. That was the nearest airport to Tiruvannamelei, my destination. I checked into a hotel put my bags in the room, and went for a walk. I saw that most of the people were walking barefooted. There did not seem to be any need for shoes in this climate. Also, instead of pants, the men wore a cloth wrapped around them from the waist down called a dhoti. It could be easily washed and dried, was cheap, and suited the hot climate. I decided that I would give up my western dress, including my shoes. I purchased a dhoti and asked the hotel manager to show me how to wear it. After he showed me, I tried many times to tie it around my waist, but as soon as I began walking it would slip off, leaving me standing in the hotel lobby in my underwear! With some effort I did finally succeed in making it stay on for longer periods.

Next came getting accustomed to Indian food. I had never eaten a red chili in my life. Though the name means cold, it is in fact anything but that! Also, 99 percent of the people in India eat with their hands, not with a knife or fork. They say that using silverware to eat is like using an interpreter in a love affair! The waiter in the restaurant asked me if I would like a spoon but I refused. I shyly observed how the other people were eating and tried it myself. I must say that I got more food into my mouth than when using chopsticks, but that is not saying much. The waiter repeatedly pressed me to use a spoon but I was adamant. What took the man next to me 10 minutes to eat took me a half hour, not to mention the mess on the table and on my clothes. Half dead from embarrassment, I finally rose from the battlefield of the table and triumphantly went to wash my hands, glad that the worst was over and hoping that the next time would be easier!

The next morning the hotel manager told me that I could catch a bus to Tiruvannamalai every hour after 6 a.m. Fortunately, he wrote down the name of the town in the local language on a slip of paper because, he said, my pronunciation was so funny that I would probably end up in Pakistan! After paying my hotel bill, I took a cycle rickshaw to the bus stand. I showed the paper around and was directed to get into a bus. With my suitcase in one hand, the directions in the other, and my dhoti slipping off again and again, I must have presented a unique sight for my fellow passengers! Finally, the bus started and I settled into the uncomfortable bench seat, waiting for a glimpse of the holy mountain Arunachala.

Neal Rosner

Chapter 2

EMPTYING THE VESSEL:
Tiruvannamalai - 1968

One hundred twenty miles and five hours later found me at the foot of the holy mountain. According to ancient Hindu legends, this mountain was the first place on the earth's surface where God manifested Himself after creation, as a blazing pillar of Light stretching endlessly into the sky. Prayed to by His devotees to take a more gross form, He became a mountain, Arunachala, which means the Red or Fiery Mountain, red being equated with the Divine Light. Over the years, countless spiritual aspirants have made Arunachala their abode as they found it to be conducive to spiritual practice. They have left behind a prolific poetic wealth praising the power of this hill as being capable of dispelling one's spiritual ignorance and revealing the Truth shining within. In more recent times, Ramana Maharshi felt a tremendous attraction for this hill, even after his Realization, and had lived there for more than 50 years. From his own experience, he told his followers that although the Supreme is all pervading, It manifests to a special degree in certain places on earth. The influence of these places can be felt by advanced aspirants and availed for spiritual progress. Coupled with the accumulated effect of the austerities of countless sages who have lived there, Arunachala was and is an ideal place for disciplining the mind in preparation for absorption into the Real. In fact, some years ago when a group of American geologists took rock samples from the hill, they found that this hill was formed at the same time as the crust of the earth. In spite of the many upheavals and floods that have taken place on the earth's surface over the ages, Arunachala has remained untouched.

From the bus stand I could see the town nestled at the foot of the hill. In the center of town was the huge temple complex which was, until the advent of movie theaters, the focal point for the religious and social life of the people. Many festivals were held year round at which one could find music, dance, and drama. People set up stalls selling various types of food and household items including toys for children. In order to educate and enlighten the average man in morals and sublime topics and to make him aware of the meaning and purpose of life, every evening after sunset a scholar well-versed in the ancient scriptures would read some verses and give an explanation to the assembled crowd. Scholars from other places would also be invited to give discourses and debates would be arranged. In this way the ancients tried to instill sublimity into the minds of the masses, who would otherwise spend their whole time engaged in mundane affairs. Even today these activities can be seen in the Hindu temples, but attendance has greatly diminished due to the craze for modern day enjoyments and amusements. The temple dedicated to the Lord as Arunachala is one of the biggest in India, stretching 24 acres within four huge compound walls with vast towers on all sides. The size of it inspires one with a feeling of reverential awe.

Getting into a horse-drawn cart, I proceeded to Sri Ramanaaramam, Ramana's abode for more than 50 years, located about 1 1/2 miles from the town in the peaceful suburbs. Before Ramana had come there, no suburbs had even existed there. Between the town and the ashram or hermitage, was only vacant land. Beyond the ashram was the burial ground for the town's dead; the only time anyone would go there was for a funeral. Now not an inch of unoccupied land lay between the town and the burial ground. The road to the ashram was always full of bullock carts, people on bicycles, and villagers walking to and from the town. Having a rainy season of only one or two months a year, Tiruvannamalai was a hot and dusty place, but this did not detract from the feeling of its ancient holiness. I had only been in Madras, a big half-westernized city. Now I was seeing the real India, villages composed of a simple and ancient culture.

Arriving at the ashram, I was greeted by an office boy. I had sent a telegram to inform them of my arrival. I was immediately taken to a clean, neat room inside the ashram and left to myself. I looked around. The room contained a bed, a cupboard set in the wall, and a fan. This was to be my new home. Come what may, I had decided to stay here until achieving Realization of the Self. I thought of the sorrow my mother must be feeling, with me so far away. Her image floated into my mind again and again. I later learned from my spiritual guides that one can detach oneself from relatives, friends, and other human contacts, but if those people have continued thoughts about one that can distract one from meditation. One could certainly suffer from distracting thoughts about them. After I struggled with such distractions for some time, I appealed to Ramana to make my mind full of his presence alone and thoughts of the past gradually subsided.

While sitting in the room wondering what to do next, the same boy appeared and asked if I wanted to see the ashram. Eagerly I replied "yes". The ashram compound spread over about six or seven acres of land. The facilities consisted of a large dining hall and kitchen, an office and book stall, the cow shed, a school for learning the Vedas or Hindu scriptures, accommodations for male guests, and a small hospital. Ladies and families were accommodated outside the ashram complex in cottages constructed for that purpose. At Ramana's bidding, women were expected to leave the ashram premises after dark and sleep in the quarters just outside to avoid any problems which may arise through temptation on the part of either sex. Though Ramana's treatment was equal towards both men and women, he was fully aware of human weakness. Those who came to him obviously had done so in order to dedicate themselves to the task of taming the mind and senses and to go beyond them to the real Self. Sex being the most powerful force for distracting the human mind, a conducive atmosphere should be provided to minimize such possibilities. To keep the men and women separate at night seemed to be the best means.

The main attraction for me was Sri Ramana's Tomb, or Samadhi as it is called. The first time I viewed it a ritualistic worship was in progress. The Samadhi was open on all sides and surrounded only by an iron fence or grill work.

Sitting on the tomb was a large white marble lotus flower upon which rested a Sivalingam, or black oval-shaped stone about five inches long. The Hindu sages had found over the ages that the round or oval shape best represented the formless Reality as it is without a beginning or end.

Because the formless Supreme is beyond conception due to its extreme subtlety, the ancient sages felt that concentration would be very difficult if an image were not provided for the mind. By concentrating on a form representing Divinity, the mind would gradually gain in serenity and subtlety and start to perceive Divinity within itself. At that stage all the forms of the universe would appear to be imbued with Divinity as the mind had become colored by That, just as one wearing green sunglasses sees everything as green. It is a well-known fact that one's perception of the world is determined by the nature of one's psyche. When the mind becomes imbued with the Divine Presence, equal vision will naturally arise. That is to say that It will be seen everywhere. This cannot take place, of course, unless impeccable concentration is achieved. Selecting one form out of the infinite forms of the universe and visualizing Divinity within it is one means for attaining such concentration as recognized and experienced by some Realized Ones.

In the Hindu ritual, one takes God as one's beloved guest and devotedly offers numerous things to Him such as water, food, flowers, and song. The last offering is the burning of camphor before the image. Camphor, when burned, leaves no residue of ash behind. It simply and completely evaporates. While burning it before God, one should feel that one is offering one's individuality to Him. If the individuality is offered and accepted, what remains is God alone as the Essence of oneself. This is God or Self-Realization. While watching the priest burn the camphor before the Samadhi I clearly felt a living presence radiating from it, similar to the current of light which I felt during meditation except that this radiance flowed from outside of me. I felt a deep peace, and was pleasantly surprised when I discovered that this was the place where Ramana's sacred remains were buried.

From that day onwards, for the next 12 years, his Tomb

became the focal point of my life. It was there that I felt his living presence and received the answers to many doubts, merely by that presence. At this time I still was not concerned whether God existed or not. I knew that Ramana would look after me always. Gradually it dawned on me that the entity I was calling Ramana was called God, Allah, Christ, or Krishna by those of different faiths. The infinite Reality could take on any number of guises to suit the time and place in order to bless and guide the devotees.

That night, for the first time in my life, I had what I would call a vision. I had just fallen asleep. I found myself sitting on the bed as Ramana entered my room. He sat down next to me and, gently patting me on the knee said, "I'm glad that you have come." His face was ablaze with a Divine luster, and a soft blissful presence was radiating from him. I felt like a child would feel near its mother. I suddenly woke up without a trace of drowsiness remaining. My uncertain mind was reassured that I had done the right thing by leaving everything and coming to him. This was the first of many such visions to come.

Beginning the next day, I followed a daily routine consisting mostly of meditation coupled with study and yoga. I felt that I needed eight hours of sleep; thus I would go to bed at 9 o'clock and rise at 5 o'clock in the morning. After supper at 7:30 p.m., I was always sleepy by 9 o'clock unless there was something that really required my attention. I later understood that eating heavily at night brings on sleepiness due to the digestive process and that if one eats sparingly or not at all at night, five hours of sleep would be more than enough.

Most of my time was spent in the hall where Ramana had lived the last 25 years of his life, amidst an ever-increasing circle of devotees. The room had been converted into a meditation hall after his demise, and one could find people meditating there at all hours from 4 in the morning until 10 at night. I used to spend about eight hours a day there trying to meditate.

One month had passed since I had settled in the ashram when a most significant event occurred. As I was walking from my room to the meditation hall one day, my eyes fixed on the ground as usual, someone coming from the opposite direction called to me, "Say, brother, are you having a good meditation? I see you meditating every day in the hall for so many hours." When I looked up, I saw a bearded figure with such a visible glow about him that a shock went through me and I just grunted, "Um." He was also on his way somewhere and did not stop to talk to me. Although I vaguely remembered reading that saints have a divine splendor about them, I had never personally seen such a thing, or had I? When Ramana had appeared in a dream a month ago I had seen a similar luster on his face. I wondered who the familiar stranger could be, but the sight of his effulgence had so numbed my mind that I could not think clearly. I sat in the meditation hall in a stupor.

In the afternoon, an American couple visiting the ashram asked me if I would like to hear one of Ramana's disciples talk that night. I agreed to meet them after supper on the hill behind the ashram. When I reached the spot at about 8 o'clock, I was taken aback; the disciple was none other than the bearded figure I spoke with that morning. He greeted me with a big smile and asked me to sit next to him. He was talking about some philosophical topics. I asked him about the nature of a glimpse of Cosmic Consciousness and received a dramatic reply in the form of a brilliant flash of lightning which illumined the landscape for a few seconds. When I returned to my room, I spent a sleepless night in anticipation of meeting him again.

The next day found me back on the hill with my friends waiting for Ratnamji as they called him. Where had I heard that name? After thinking it over for a long time, I realized that this must be the Ratnamji that Barbara had told me about when I stayed with her in Nepal. Things started to make sense. Ratnamji soon arrived, his face beaming as usual. I have never known a person who was uniformly happy all the time until I met Ratnamji. He exuded happiness. I was eager to ask him a question which had been troubling me since I left America.

"Ratnamji, may I ask a question?"

"Yes, what is it?" he said smiling at me.

"Ever since I left America six months ago, I have felt that money is a burden. I want to become a monk, but at the same time I am keeping money in my pocket. Would it not be better if I were to give all my money to an ashram and live there peacefully the rest of my life?" I asked.

"Brother, you are just starting your spiritual life and do not have the internal wealth of spiritual practice. When you have that, you will always be provided for by God. Even if you gave your money to an ashram, how long would they let you stay? Perhaps after a few months they would want more money and, if you did not have more, they would ask you to leave. Then what would you do? Still, it is quite easy to live without money. It is just a matter of getting used to it and adapting your needs to with whatever you receive. There is nothing very great or difficult in it. But it is much more difficult to keep some money and spend it freely without calculating how much is left and how more will come. The urge to live makes food a necessity, and money is desired to buy food. The attachment to money is like the clinging to life. In fact, we could even call money the external life breath of a worldly man. If it is taken away, he feels as if choked to death. If one spends without attachment, however, one can observe how one's mind is acting and slowly root out any attachment which may be lurking within. If I were you, I would continue my meditation and at the same time spend the money without worrying about the future."

I was impressed by his practical knowledge of spiritual life and the workings of the mind. I was relieved of my burden. A deep reverence and love welled up in my heart for this wise man, as simple and happy as a child, but deep in wisdom as a sage. I relished his company like a starving man with a sumptuous meal. I wondered how I could develop a closer relationship with him. I did not even know where he was staying or how he spent his time. After hearing him talk to my friends, we parted.

The next night I had laid down to sleep around 9 o'clock. At 11 o'clock I heard a knock on the door. I did not want to be disturbed and so I did not get up or answer. After a few moments there was a knock on the window next to my bed.

"Neal, Neal! Are you awake?"

"No!" I answered back a bit irritated.

"Open the door. I'm hungry," said the voice.

Reluctantly, I got up and opened the door. Ratnamji walked in.

"I had to go to the town tonight to meet some devotees there. Their father had recently died and they wanted me to come and sing the Divine Name and give them a little consolation. I'm having gastric trouble and if I do not eat now and then it increases. Do you have anything to eat with you?" He was looking at me intently, which I surmised was to see if I was angry at being awakened.

I had some peanuts and raw sugar in my room. I brought it out and gave him some of it, keeping back the rest for myself. It happened to be his favorite snack! He kept asking for more and more, until I was chagrined to see that all of it was eaten. He went on talking about what he had told the people in the town in order to comfort them and other small but very educative talk. He was all the time watching me closely. I was still thinking about going back to sleep, but he would not leave until after 1 o'clock. I felt a peculiar bliss while sitting with him but my resentment at having been disturbed and the desire to resume sleep was marring it.

I did not suspect that he was testing me to gauge my mental makeup. Did I really want to become a monk, or did I want to cling to things other than the Real? He knew the way to find out. Just the previous day I was asking about renunciation of money, and now I was concerned because my stock of peanuts had been eaten. I was already calculating how much money I would have to spend on peanuts and raw sugar if he were to come every night and how much money would be left over! Here was my first practical lesson in spending without attachment and I had, of course, failed miserably.

Ratnamji was staying in a room in the ashram hospital. He was assisting the head priest in the daily worship conducted at Ramana's Samadhi. Because of this service, he was given a room so that he need not leave the ashram many times a day to rest. There was worship three times a day, which meant that most of his day was spent cleaning, bringing water, arranging offerings, and keeping everything ready for the next worship.

On the day after Ratnamji had eaten my peanuts, he

came to my room and laid down on the floor. There was no fan in his room, and the heat of the day was quite unbearable. He thought he could make use of my fan, and we could spend some time together. Due to a false sense of superiority, I resented his intruding on my privacy, but at the same time I did enjoy his company. I lay down on the bed, and he was on the floor. I was so dull-minded and irreverent at that time that I did not offer my bed to him. He was about 48 at that time and I was 19. Because I had always lived in America, I did not know how one should act in the presence of saints, and even if I had known, I probably would not have acted properly due to arrogance and laziness.

At that time, I thought very highly of myself for having left my home and, because I could do a few yogic postures and some meditation, I felt that I was already a full-blown yogi! It had never occurred to me that a real yogi is full of humility due to experiencing the presence of the impersonal Reality within himself. He realizes that his personality or individuality is nothing, a mere shadowy appearance subject to constant change, and that the impersonal Being which is the basis of the individual is alone real and unchanging. The waves belong to the ocean and not the other way around. The waves come and go but the ocean remains the same. A real mahatma or great soul is one who feels that he is nothing and that God, or the Universal Self, alone is real.

I asked Ratnamji how he came to Ramana. His reply came in the form of a fantastic story. Seeing his sincerity, I could not doubt the truth of it.

"When I was 18," he began, "I had just completed my schooling and been awarded a Bachelor of Science degree and also a scholarship to continue my studies. I was a very good student. At that time I started to suffer from a mysterious kind of disease. I developed an unquenchable thirst and had to drink huge quantities of water all day long. When I say huge, I mean in the neighborhood of 15 to 20 gallons or about three to four buckets of water in 24 hours. This was strange enough, but the most unusual thing was that I would pass only the normal quantity of urine. Though drinking 20 gallons of water a day, I was passing only a pint or so of urine. I also felt severe pain in the bottom of my spine. My relatives took me to every kind of doctor—herbal, homeopathic, allopathic, and various country physicians—but to no avail. They could find neither the cause nor the cure. Finally, I was admitted to Madras Government Hospital about 500 miles away from my own village. A cousin of mine accompanied me there.

"After a stay of two months, I was discharged in quite the same condition. The doctors were nonplussed by my case. I was becoming weaker day by day and finally decided to go home and await death. My cousin and I got on a train and traveled to a place about 150 miles away from my village where another cousin lived. We decided to eat lunch there and spent the night before proceeding to our village the next day. On reaching the house, we were greeted by my cousin who asked why we were coming from Madras. On hearing about my condition he told me, "There is a man visiting this town now who, people say, is able to cure many kinds of apparently incurable diseases. Shall we go and see him before you go? He's not a doctor, but I have heard that he goes into a trance and then prescribes some remedies. Shall we go?" Having tried everything else, I thought "Why not? What can I lose?" After lunch we went to see the gentleman.

As soon as I walked into the room, the man exclaimed, "Ratnamji has come! Call him here immediately!" I was, of course, surprised, to say the least! How could he have known my name? Nobody there expected or knew us. I went close to him and saw that he was sitting on the ground with an image of Hanuman before him. The image had been decorated with flowers, and a huge heap of betel leaves lay before it."

"Who is Hanuman?" I queried.

"There is an ancient work called the *Ramayana* which is the life story of Sri Rama who is considered to be an Incarnation of God in India just as Christ is in the west. The Hindus believe that God incarnates numberless times in the course of human history in order to set man on the right path leading to His Realization. He corrects the evil doers and helps the virtuous. He incarnates in all parts of the world as He feels the need or sends His close devotees or saints to this world to do the work, endowing them with Divine power. Thousands of years ago Sri Rama took birth in North India and enacted His life drama. Hanuman was one of His faithful servants and devotees of the nonhuman realm. He was a monkey, but a very intelligent and faithful one. In fact, according to the *Ramayana*, he was a portion of Divinity Itself who came down to take part in Sri Rama's Divine drama, and he is worshipped as such even today. It has been found that his worship is very efficacious in dispelling evil spirits."

"What do you mean 'evil spirits'?" I asked Ratnamji. "Do you really believe that such things exist?"

"Well, like you, I was also very rational concerning spiritual and religious things in those days. Unless I experienced it directly, I would not take anything for granted. I even wrote a paper condemning the traditional viewpoint on certain Hindu beliefs and customs."

Ratnamji continued, "What happened soon convinced me of the truth that there is more than what meets the eye. Hanumadass, as this gentleman was called, motioned to me to come near. He closed his eyes and then slowly, in a whisper, told me that I was not having a disease but that the problem was something else and that by Hanuman's grace it would go away. There was a new Hanuman temple in the town. He asked me to walk around it 100 times every day without fail for one month and then to come back to him. When he told me to go around the temple, he said 'Go around my temple,' so that I should understand that Hanuman Himself was talking to me.

"Not very impressed, we left the place and returned to my cousin's house. I had already spent so much time with doctors and in hospitals that I thought what does it matter if I try this for a month? Even if nothing comes of it, I have spent my time in a good way worshipping God in the form of Hanuman. I resolved to start going round the temple the next day.

"The next morning found me at Hanuman's temple. There was a path around it especially designed for those who chose to worship by circumambulation. Praying to Hanuman for success in the undertaking, I did the 100 rounds and returned home. That night immediately after falling asleep, I dreamt that Hanuman stood in a tiny form by the side of my bed. He smiled and motioned towards the opposite side of the bed. Looking there, I saw a thin, ghostly figure. I felt a bit frightened. Then the figure vanished. I woke up and found that Hanuman was still standing by my bed! Within a few seconds, the figure of Hanuman also gradually faded away. I could not sleep for the rest of the night but sat up repeating the name of Hanuman and meditating.

"After the sun rose, I went to Hanumadass's house and told him of my experience the previous night. He was not in trance and told me there was nothing to worry about. I was possessed by a ghost who was using my body to satisfy its intense thirst. By showing His form, Hanuman was reassuring me that He would get rid of the parasite. Such had been the case with many, I was told.

"I continued circumambulation of the temple for 29 days, but the thirst did not decrease at all. My faith was faltering. But when I woke up on the 30th morning the thirst had vanished. That whole day I waited to see what would happen, but I felt perfectly normal and even the pain in my spine had subsided. I was elated. After going to the temple, I went to Hanumadass and told him the good news. I asked if he would initiate me into the worship and mantra of Hanuman, to which he agreed. I lived with him and his wife almost as their own child. I traveled with him to different villages, assisting him in his work of removing evil spirits. I helped in the daily worship, cooking the food offering and whatever else I was allowed to do.

"One day we were requested to come to a village where a young woman of about 26 was thought to be possessed. She frequently talked in fluent English, a language unknown to her. When we arrived, we were taken to the girl's house and she was brought in. Hanumadass asked her who she was. There was no reply. He repeated the question and reassured her that he had not come to hurt her. She began to speak in perfect English.

"She said, 'I was a college student who used to pass by this house every day while going to school and was enamoured by the beauty of this girl. I had a strong desire to enjoy her company, but this of course was impossible un-

less we were to get married. Suddenly one day I was involved in a fatal accident and died. Now I am enjoying her
in a subtle form. If you think that Hanuman can get rid of me
you are mistaken. I will not go so easily as my friend had
gone from Ratnamji's body!'

"I was amazed, to say the least, to hear those words.
Apparently, these beings lived in a common world unseen
by humans. By following certain rites, however, Hanumadass soon relieved the girl of the possession.

"I had spent about two years with Hanumadass, when
one day Hanumadass called me while he was in trance. He
told me that in southern India there was a great sage named
Ramana Maharshi and that I should go there and live near
him and by serving him, attain to the real goal of life, Realization of my True Nature. Neither Hanumadass nor I had
heard of this sage. We made inquiries and finally learned
that he was staying at the foot of Arunachala in a town
called Tiruvannamalai. Bidding farewell to my first master
and his wife, I proceeded to Arunachala.

"When I came here I directly entered the hall where
Ramana was sitting on his sofa. He beckoned me to sit
down. I bowed to him and sat on the floor. Closing my
eyes, I started to repeat the mantra which I had learned
from Hanumadass but strangely enough, I could not remember it! I had repeated it thousands of times over the
past two years but now I had totally forgotten it. The next
moment, I felt the consciousness of my body disappearing,
and in its place was a vast ocean of radiant light. My mind
was perfectly still and filled with an ineffable peace and
light. I do not know how long I remained like that.

"Finally, after some time I opened my eyes and found
that Ramana was gazing at me with a smile on his lips. I
bowed down to him and left the hall. Whenever I sat in his
presence during the next few days, the same experience
repeated itself. I felt that I belonged here and wished to
make this place my permanent home. I hoped to settle in the
ashram. I did, however, feel that I needed the permission of
my mother before settling here permanently. I left the Maharshi and returned home by train. As I rode in the train, I
felt the same peace and light I had experienced in the hall. I
reached my village and told my mother what had hap-

pened. She shed tears of joy and said, 'My child, I also wished to lead a life of renunciation and spirituality, but somehow I got married. I was disappointed that none of my nine children had a similar aspiration. They are all content to lead worldly lives. Only you, the youngest, are the answer to my prayers. My life's desire to live as a nun will find its fulfillment through you. Go, my son. Your father is Ramana and your real home is Arunachala. He is calling you. You have my full blessings.'

"I then returned here and gradually was accepted into Ramana's personal service. That was about 20 years ago."

By the time Ratnamji finished narrating this story, it was time for him to leave, as he followed a strict routine. He got up and left and I followed him. I wanted to see how he spent his time. In the evening, he cleaned the shrine, or Samadhi, joined in the chanting of the Vedas, took part in the worship, and then went off by himself for about two hours to meditate. After dinner he would meet with visiting devotees, study, or walk around the Arunachala hill alone or in the company of others. He would never sleep before 11 o'clock. He got up each morning at 3:30 and followed a similar routine of cleaning the shrine, worship, and meditation until lunch. He also had his own private worship, or puja, as it is called, which he would do in his room. I watched him for some days and wondered how he could manage with only 41/2 hours of sleep. Finally I approached him with a request which, unknown to me, would transform my whole life.

"Ratnamji. You seem to be straining yourself so much. Is there any work I could do which would relieve you of some of your burden?" I questioned him.

"Well, why don't you start with picking flowers for the morning worship? You must give them to me by 6 a.m. In order to finish in time, you should start the work by 4:30. Before that, it is best for you to attend to your nature calls, clean your teeth, and take your bath. Then you will be in a fit condition to do Divine service."

Work must start by 4:30? That means I must get up by 4 o'clock. It is surprising to find that the apparently indispensable and impossible-to-give-up sleep in the early morning is easily shaken off when necessity arises. If one has to catch a plane at 5 a.m., would he not get up by 3:30? In fact, many of our so-called necessities are merely unnecessary habits. Most of us sleep too much, eat too much, talk too much, and worry too much, thinking that it is all very necessary.

I quickly learned that one can reduce life's necessities to the barest minimum to conserve energy and in no way harm one's body. Our life span and energy, if properly used, can take us to the spiritual goal in this life itself. Due to our squandering life force in excessive sleeping and other unnecessary activities, we fail to attain what we have set out to achieve. It is not uncommon to come across people who have been meditating for 20 or 30 years but have made no appreciable progress, nor have they gained any spiritual experience apart from a little peace of mind, fragile though it may be. If one looked closely at their inner lives one would find they had squandered their energy, through ignorance or carelessness, and had frustrated the purpose of life. If we want water to reach the upper stories of a house quickly, we should make sure that the taps downstairs are closed. Likewise, if we wish to gain spiritual progress quickly, we should be very economical with our energy so the life force can rise higher and higher towards the top of the head through concentration, ultimately merging in the Supreme.

It was the middle of winter and although hot in the day, it was very cool at night. In the early morning, the temperature was perhaps 50 degrees. Not knowing that hot water was available in the ashram bathroom, I kept a stock of water overnight in a drum in my attached bath. Pouring that ice cold water over my body in that cool morning breeze was a shortcut for going beyond body-consciousness! After bathing and dressing, I took a basket into the large ashram flower garden. Although it was pleasant to pick flowers from the extensive garden, in the early morning, there was one hitch. The whole area was infested with scorpions and various kinds of snakes ranging from harmless water snakes to king cobras. Carrying a flashlight was not possible because both hands were needed for the work and the only light was a dim 25 watt bulb in a veranda about 50 yards away.

Here was a real lesson in surrender to the Master. Was my mind on the flowers or on the snakes? Gradually, I did develop enough trust in Ramana that I did not even think of the snakes and scorpions. I was never bitten or stung by anything more poisonous than a honey bee or mosquito. On some mornings, there was a torrential downpour as the monsoon season had just started. Downpour or not, the flowers must reach the shrine by 6 a.m. sharp. I thought of purchasing an umbrella but Ratnamji would not hear of it. He said that since I wanted to become a monk, I must do with the barest minimum. He showed me how to tie a dhoti in such a way that it served the purpose of an umbrella, something like a poncho but of cotton.

While picking flowers, I noticed a peculiar fact about how my mind worked. Even before picking one flower, my eye was on the next one. I was surprised at my lack of concentration. Picking flowers actually became a lesson in concentration and surrender, not to mention patience. After delivering the flowers at the Samadhi, I still had the urge for more work. Ratnamji said that I could sweep the area around the shrine and wash the front steps leading into it. I am left-handed, so when I picked up the broom and started to sweep he noticed that I was using what he said was the wrong hand and, in spite of my protests, insisted that only the right hand be used at least while doing Divine service. I asked him if it was not a bit old-fashioned to consider the left hand as the wrong one. He replied that the ancient sages were not fools. Their vision was one of omniscience. They saw that the left hand had a negative vibration and should be used only as an assistant to the right one. If I doubted the sages, I could, of course, do as I liked.

As I was not so bold as to do that, I struggled to learn sweeping with my right hand. Another problem was that the broom was only about 11/2 feet long. It was a very old worn-out one, and I had to bend over in order to sweep properly. The area in front of the shrine was big. Even with a good broom it would take about half an hour to clean it. With the short broom, it took me nearly 45 minutes and I panted for breath afterwards. I ventured to ask for a better broom.

"We are poor monks and have to do with the minimum. If necessary, Ramana will supply a better one automatically. Until then you work with this one," came the reply.

I started to wonder what I had gotten myself into by offering to help with Ratnamji's work, but I could not back out so soon after having taken it up, so I continued.

Whenever he had a few minutes of leisure, Ratnamji came to my room and to talk. He told me about his life with Ramana, who had been a strict disciplinarian with his close disciples. He, of course, showed much affection to all of them and concern for their spiritual progress. For those who were really serious about gaining spiritual experience, he was very strict about all details. A stub of pencil should not be thrown away, even if a new pencil was available, because everything was provided by God and should be used fully and properly. Even waste paper should be used at least for lighting the fire, not just thrown away. Ramana would cut off the blank edges of a newspaper and, binding them together, use them for writing small verses or notes. He taught by example that one should take the minimum for oneself and give the maximum to others. Even on his death bed, when taking his last breath, he insisted that those who had come to see him should be allowed to do so. His was a selfless and desireless existence, and he expected the same from his disciples.

In those days there were four or five men attending Ramana in shifts. When Ratnamji joined the ashram, they asked him which shift he preferred. He replied that he would take whatever was remaining after they had all made their choices. Of course, nobody wanted the night shift from 10 p.m. to 4 a.m., as that meant no sleep. This shift was given to Ratnamji. He said that because he had put himself last and was ready to take the worst part, he actually got the best because at night no one would be in the ashram and he would be alone with Ramana in the hall. Ramana slept very little, and he taught Ratnamji many things. There was also no one else around. In a very short time Ratnamji learned more from Ramana than would be possible in many years.

By talking to me and sharing his experiences, Ratnamji made me feel that I was his own child or a younger brother.

He also asked me about my past and suggested many things in matters of diet, yoga postures, and meditation. Gradually our relationship deepened. It slowly dawned on me that Ratnamji was the answer to my prayer for a Guru. He had been meticulously trained by Ramana and was a wise man in his own right. I went to him one day and told him,

"I feel that you are my Guru."

"You are mistaken," he said, "you and I have the same Guru. That is Ramana Maharshi. As far as I am concerned, you are my younger spiritual brother."

I felt disappointed and it obviously showed on my face.

"Well, if it will make you feel better, you can consider me as an instrument of Ramana's given to you by Him in order to show you the way. But I must warn you now. In my 28 years here, I have never met a single person who was able to keep up with me. I have to maintain the standard shown to me by my Guru, and those who want to move with me will have to do the same. I have never chased anyone away, but most have gone of their own accord because they couldn't keep up with my pace."

I decided then and there that, even if I should die in the attempt, I would never leave him or fall by the wayside. I asked him what were the duties of a disciple.

"After developing faith in a Master, one should implicitly obey whatever he may say knowing that it is only with your spiritual betterment in mind that he asks you to do anything in a particular way. If you don't have full faith in a saint, it is better not to take him as your Master, but if you do, you must be unquestioningly obedient. Even in worldly knowledge, you must follow the instructions of your teachers in order to learn and get the desired results. This is much more so if you want spiritual experience, which is far more subtle and complex than worldly knowledge."

Obedience. Though I knew the meaning of the word, I had no practical experience. From my childhood onwards I consistently disobeyed my mother, my teachers, and society. Mine was a life of anarchy—to do as I like when and how I liked. I could, however, understand that one must obey prescribed rules to achieve a particular goal. I wanted the experience of Absolute Bliss, and I felt that Ratnamji had it and was willing to show me the way to attain it. Certainly it would be no great difficulty to obey him. However, for the next eight years of our relationship, until his demise, obedience was my main spiritual practice and struggle.

One who is obedient to a real sage slowly attains real peace of mind. The same God-conscious state experienced by the sage is gradually experienced by oneself. It is something like tuning a radio. The numerous radio waves pervade the atmosphere, but we will hear only those to which our radio is tuned. Our minds are like a radio in continuously receiving gross stimuli through the five senses and, subtly, through the minds and vibrations of other living beings. The subtlest of all principles is, of course, the Truth, or God. It has been told to us by those who have experienced it that God can be known only when the mind becomes extremely subtle, pure, and serene. To reach that state requires continuous training and uncompromising supervision by one who knows God perfectly. Our actions and speech follow the dictates of our mind. One's mental condition can be fairly well judged when one's words and actions are observed although there are such things as hidden motives which we need not consider now. Spiritual aspirants through the ages have also learned that one can alter one's mental condition by changing one's actions and words.

This is the essence of the relationship between a real sage and a sincere disciple. The disciple desires the experience of Reality, but due to erroneous thinking and acting, that experience is impossible to attain unless the errors of his ways are pointed out and corrected. When the mind is purified, the in-dwelling Truth will shine forth spontaneously, free from obstructing forces. A real saint merely points out one's errors and helps one to correct oneself. When the mind has reached its pure or correct condition, everything will be achieved effortlessly in a moment. Though the advice of the Master may at times make no sense, when one's spiritual experience deepens one can fully understand the significance of such instructions. Until then, obedience is the only way.

Today, there are many cults and self-proclaimed Gurus. I am not referring to them. My concern is only with a sincere aspirant for Self-Knowledge and a genuine sage living in that state. Of course, each one must observe and try to judge whether a particular individual is fit to be a guide on the spiritual path, although it is admittedly very difficult to judge whether another is enlightened or not. Although fearlessness, selflessness, absence of sensuality and a sense of equality towards all are some of the distinguishing characteristics of a Realized Soul, they may not always manifest in an obvious way. Ultimately, our intuition must decide. It seems to be Nature's Law that a sincere aspirant does eventually gain the company of a real saint though there may be some delay.

About one month after I met Ratnamji, I realized that my daily routine had changed drastically. What had started out as a little help to relieve him of his burden came to be a full time job. I had practically no time to sit and meditate. As my love and admiration for him increased so also did the time I spent with him until I was moving with him 24 hours a day. I closely observed his way of life and his words to me and others. He told me many times that I should not accept anything he said simply because it was he that said it. I should reflect deeply on whether or not it was correct and, if there was any doubt, I should ask him. With this wonderful man there was neither spoon-feeding nor dictatorship. He wanted me to develop through my own intelligence. He was the guide, but I was the driver.

Though he never asked me to do anything of my own accord, I expanded my work from picking flowers and sweeping to cleaning his room, arranging his personal puja, bringing hot water for his bath in the morning, acting as secretary for his English correspondence, and various other jobs. I reduced my sleep to five hours and felt none the worse for it. If anything, I was more fresh and alert. Also, I found that eating two square meals a day without anything in between was more than enough and kept my body light. If I felt that Ratnamji needed food, I purchased it unasked by him. His needs were extremely minimal.

I started to sleep on the floor as he was doing and found it more comfortable than a bed. Once one gets used to a simple life, one can live anywhere happily, even if one has nothing. Because we cannot get some of our so-called necessities we suffer no end of mental worry and agitation. If a luxurious room with a thick mattress, a TV and attached bathroom are not available, many of us feel as if life is unbearable! Actually, six feet of space anywhere, even under a tree, is quite enough for anyone who is healthy. The attitude of the mind makes all the difference.

One day a post card came for Ratnamji inviting him to attend a big function at an ashram in north India. Printed at the top of the card was a mantra of the Divine Name. Under that was a quotation from one of the Hindu scriptures praising the power of that mantra. It said that if one repeated it 35 million times, one's mind would attain absolute purity and merge into the Real. I asked Ratnamji if it were so.

"Of course it's so. The Scriptures were compiled by ancient sages who had all realized God through various means. They were scientists who experimented with various spiritual practices obtaining the results of God Realization. They handed down the information to their disciples, who in turn handed them down to their disciples, and so forth. This was all done by word of mouth. In ancient days, there were no printing presses and knowledge was passed on in the oral tradition. Because they followed a disciplined life, they had tremendous memory power and could remember whatever was taught even if it was thousands of verses.

"The Scriptures are the record of those ancient sages' spiritual experiences. Of course, years ago those verses were compiled, written down, and distributed through mass circulation. Some years ago, I witnessed a Vedic scholar recite by heart a portion of the Veda which took him 28 hours! Not only must the verses be correct but every syllable must be intoned in a particular way or the meaning may change. Even in the present day, there are scholars with this superb memory power."

Hearing these words, I decided that I would repeat the mantra 35 million times. I calculated that if I repeated it at moderate speed for 18 hours a day, even while doing other things, it would take about 25 years to complete. I asked Ratnamji whether he thought it was a good idea and he approved. From that moment onwards, I took that as my main practice to realize God.

After I had been in the ashram for two months, some difficulties started to arise. Some of the other sadhus, or monks, residing there started to have feel jealous of Ratnamji, thinking that perhaps I was giving him large sums of money. In India westerners are usually thought to be rich by the natives, and they may be rich in comparison with the Indians. In truth I had never given Ratnamji any money and, apart from some food, I did not purchase anything for him. Now and then, I was warned not to associate with him to which I strongly objected. This only made things worse until one day I was asked to leave my room and move into the general guest room with the rest of the visiting monks. I told Ratnamji and he suggested that I look for a room outside the ashram for it would only be a matter of time until I would be asked to leave. I searched in the colony surrounding the ashram and found a large room for a very reasonable rate at the very first house where I inquired. That same day, I shifted my few belongings to the new room and thus began a new chapter in my training.

This house belonged to one of the oldest devotees of Ramana. He had been living there since the 1930's along with his family. He also happened to be a close friend of Ratnamji, who had lived in his house about 20 years earlier. He was a very saintly and childlike person who was always ready to tell captivating stories about his life with Ramana. The house was a five-minute walk from the ashram and was surrounded by a big garden of nearly one acre with many fruit and flower trees. It was the ideal place to lead a secluded life of spiritual practice. Narayana, as he was called, told me that when he wanted to dig a well for the house he took a ground plan of his land to Ramana and asked him where he should dig the well. Ramana put his finger on one spot and the well was dug there. During the hot season almost every well in the area would dry up except for this one and the well in the ashram which remained at least half full, both being fed by a perennial spring.

Narayana had come as a skeptic to Ramana only on the insistence of a friend. When he entered the hall, Ramana was discussing a point from the Vedantic Scriptures which speak of the oneness of God and His creation. He was saying that one who, after purifying the mind, had attained identity with God was, even though endowed with a body, in no way different from the Formless Absolute. The Power of the Supreme is manifested in such a being.

Narayana waited until Ramana came out of the hall, on the way to take his meal, and asked him, "You were speaking about the identity of God and a Liberated One. Are you speaking from your own experience?"

Ramana gave a gentle smile and replied, "Would I say such a thing without having experienced it? "Hearing those words Narayana was overwhelmed with a feeling of reverence and prostrated like a log of wood on the ground before the Maharshi and thenceforth became one of the inner circle of his devotees.

Within a few days of my moving to the new room, Ratnamji came to see the place. After exchanging greetings with Narayana, he had a look around the room. He said that it would be better to cook my own food than take from the family. It would be cheaper and would be a great help for my spiritual life. According to Ratnamji, food once cooked becomes sensitive to those who handle it. Like a magnet, it picks up and retains vibrations. If those who handle the food are full of negative thoughts, some of those thoughts will find their way into our minds after ingesting the food. The subtle thoughts affect the subtle part of our body, the mind, while the gross part goes to build the physical body. This has little bearing on worldly people as they are not very concerned with molding the contents of their minds.

A spiritual aspirant, however, must be very careful to reduce and purify his thoughts. Only in the absolutely thoughtfree mind can the Real Self shine forth unobstructed. By cooking for oneself, one gradually becomes able to ascertain which are one's own thoughts and which are the thoughts of others. When maximum time is spent trying to tame and concentrate the mind, one comes to see the value of it. He also said that one should not hesitate to accept food from someone who has attained a higher level of spiritual realization than oneself as that will help one spiritually. He told me to purchase a cheap kerosene stove and some earthen warepots along with raw food stuffs.

The next day I went to the market and purchased all the required things. Around 10 o'clock Ratnamji came after completing his work in the ashram. I was told to bring water, and after I put it on the stove, he showed me how to cut the vegetables. He said, "In India we use only one vegetable as a side dish per day and change it every day. Rice or wheat is the staple food so cooking can be very easy. Just cook the rice in one pot. Then put some lentils in another pot and after boiling them until they are soft, throw in the vegetable and add spices and salt. If you like, purchase some milk and make it into yogurt to be mixed with the food. For variety, you can change the vegetable every day. This may not be the way family people cook, being very minimal, but for us it will be enough. If you want to simplify the mind, you must simplify everything about your external life. This may be boring for ordinary people, but it is a minute by minute adventure for an aspirant to see how far he can reduce the flow of thoughts."

"Why are you cutting the vegetable so slowly? If you do like that it will be tomorrow by the time we get lunch ready!" he exclaimed.

I felt that I was cutting quite quickly and told him so. He took the knife from my hand and finished the work in half the time that it would have taken me to do it.

"One can be careful and at the same time be quick. In the name of carefulness one should not be a slowpoke. Serenity and dullness look the same from the outside to a superficial observer. You must understand the difference between the two and throw slowness to a distance. A devotee must be quick and efficient and at the same time he should not lose his peace of mind. He should be able to turn out as much or more work as others but not feel any mental fatigue. I remember one day when I was massaging Ramana's knee joints with some medicated oil. He had severe rheumatism and required daily massaging. As I was rubbing his knees I started to huff and puff. He told me to stop. 'Because you are identifying with the work so much, your life breath is getting agitated. When you do work, don't let your mind get attached to it. Try to remain mentally aloof as a witness, calm and cool within, even though working like a madman without,' he advised me.

"I tried it and now I am able to do any amount of work without mental fatigue or increase of thoughts. If I sit for meditation my mind immediately sinks to the bottom and gets merged into its source. If I work with attachment and agitation, it becomes impossible to meditate for many hours afterwards until the momentum of the thought waves slows down. Though you may not be detached now, at least repeat the Divine Name while working. Gradually, even though you are working, your mind will cling to the Name instead of the work, and your peace will not be disturbed."

He called me over to his side and, pointing at the pot of boiling vegetable pieces, he said, "See, because of the heat the vegetable pieces are jumping and dancing. If I remove the pot everything will be quiet. The mind is like that. By doing work with attachment, you get your mind heated up and your thoughts start to jump and dance. No heat, no dancing!"

Everything seemed to be an opportunity for Ratnamji to teach me some spiritual principle. Being with him meant continuous learning. I had played truant from school many times when younger. Now I was paying for it by receiving lessons day and night.

I sat in the corner to see what was next. He took the pots from the fire and put some food on my plate and then on another plate for himself. Then he asked me if I had a photo of Ramana. I had a book with Ramana's photo in it and brought it. He placed it near the food and slowly pretended to be feeding the photo. This went on for about 15 seconds and then he took some of the food outside and gave it to some hungry dogs and crows that were waiting there. After that we both sat down to eat.

"What was all that?" I asked him.

"We are looking upon Ramana as our Guru and God. By feeding him first the food will become holy and will help us to conquer our minds. Most westerners do not like the idea of worshipping a man as God or, for that matter, ascribing any kind of form to the Formless One. This probably has come from the teaching in the Old Testament that God should not be worshipped in any form, that He has a personality but no form. In the Vedic religion, God in His absolute aspect has neither form nor personality. He is Pure Being, best expressed in the words 'I am that I am' as told to Moses on Sinai by the Lord. However, for purposes of worship and communion with His devotees He can and does manifest His Presence in any object of this universe. If one's devotion and thoughts are strong enough, one can see Him pervading every atom of creation.

"As the thinker pervades his thoughts, God pervades this universe which is nothing but a product of His Will or Thought. If we want to see God within and merge our mind into Him, thereby attaining Divine Bliss, we need to concentrate and make the mind subtle. How does one concentrate on a formless, skylike Being? Our mind is continuously occupied with forms and sounds. We must choose one form and try to see God in it. Gradually, concentration will be achieved and we will be able to see Him in everything as the all-pervading Essence. That is why I first offered the food to God in the form of our Guru and then in the form of some hungry animals. We will get a feeling of sympathy and oneness with other beings which will eventually expand our vision to the Universal Vision of God in all. Do you understand?"

In answering a simple question, Ratnamji had covered the whole range of Semitic and Oriental philosophy in a nutshell! I was wonderstruck at his depth of learning and broadness of views.

After we finished our meal, he laid down on a mat to rest. I started to clean up the corner of the room we had used as a kitchen. I squatted as I removed the plates and pots.

"Why do you squat like that?" he remarked. "If you stand up and bend at the waist to do the work on the ground, you will stretch your leg muscles and make your nerves stronger, which in turn will remove the dullness of your nervous system. If dullness and restlessness are both removed, meditation will flow easily." I did as he said and went out to clean the pots. I took some soap powder and started to scrub the pots standing, of course, and bending at the waist.

"See, we are monks and we cannot afford to use soap in such a wasteful way. If you take some dry, soft sand and use it instead of soap, it will remove the oil and dirt and will not cost us anything. Yesterday I saw you cleaning a bottle which had contained oil. You wasted so much soap. If you just pour dry sand into it, shake it up and stick a twig inside it and twist it around, all of the oil sticking to the sides will be removed. Then, just a bit of soap is necessary to make it absolutely clean."

I was starting to feel a little choked up. It seems that I did not know how to do anything properly and that he knew everything. I was afraid to move an inch lest even my walking should prove to be wrong! I finished washing the utensils and put them on the shelf. He looked to see if I had put them with their mouths facing down. Fortunately I had that much common sense. I laid down and started to fall asleep.

"Hey, Neal! Sleeping? It's not so good to sleep in the daytime. If you sleep after sunrise or before sunset, the body gets overheated and, instead of feeling refreshed, you will feel drowsy and jaded. If you're feeling tired you can just wash your face and arms and lie down for some time repeating the Divine Name, but don't close your eyes!"

Perhaps I should not breathe, I thought.

In the afternoon, Ratnamji went back to the ashram to continue his work there. After some time I followed and, after attending the Vedic chanting and evening worship at the Samadhi, I went for meditation. While meditating I felt uncontrollably sleepy and my head nodded moments after I closed my eyes. I tried to throw off the sleep but could not. I felt disappointed and went back to my room and finished what was left of the midday meal. Ratnamji had cooked enough so that I need not cook again at night.

He came to the room about 8 p.m. after finishing his meal in the ashram. He brought a friend with him, a tall stout man with a radiant smile on his face and a ready childlike laugh. He might have been in his late sixties.

"This is Bhaiji," he said. "Bhaiji was one of the first people I met when I came here in 1942. He is a retired philosophy professor from Hyderabad, a big city about 500 miles north of here. Since the thirties he has been coming to Ramana whenever he can spare time from his professional or family duties. Ever since we met, we have liked each other, and he has acted as a father, mother, older brother, and guide to me all these years, something like you and me. Bhaiji, tell Neal how you came to Ramana.

"I was teaching philosophy in the biggest university in the state at that time," Bhaiji said. "I was about 42 years old. Although interested in spiritual life at an early age, I had not dedicated myself to it heart and soul. One day while taking a shower, at home I heard a sound and turned around. I saw a man standing in the bathroom looking at me, smiling. I was sure I had locked the bathroom door. The man had nothing on except a loin cloth and was holding a walking stick in one hand. I felt frightened and, screaming in terror, I rushed out of the bathroom. My family came running. Upon hearing the reason for my uproar, they searched the bathroom but could find no trace of the stranger.

"About one week later, I was looking through a book on nondualistic philosophy, and was quite surprised to find on the front page a picture of the man I had seen in my bathroom, loin cloth, walking stick, and all. Under the photo was his name, Sri Ramana Maharshi. The introduction to the book explained that he was an Enlightened Sage living at the foot of Arunachala. As soon as I could get leave from my job, I went to Arunachala.

"Upon reaching the ashram, I walked directly into the hall. Ramana was sitting on the sofa radiating a palpable peace around him. He gave me a piercing but, at the same time, gracious glance and laughingly exclaimed, 'Even before coming here he has seen Ramana!' From that moment I became dedicated wholeheartedly to achieving the spiritual Goal and became devoted to him as my Guru and guide."

Before Bhaiji left, he took me aside and told me that I was really fortunate to have Ratnamji as a guide on the spiritual path. He explained to me that Ratnamji was a saint of a high order and that I should not be fooled by his humble appearance and actions. He then took leave of us and returned to the ashram. It was about 11 o'clock by that time. I felt sleepy and was about to lie down. Ratnamji, who was already lying down, called me and told me that it would be better to clean the remaining one or two pots now so that time could be saved tomorrow. Grudgingly I did as he said, then started to lie down again, all the time thinking that I must get up at 3:30 the next morning. I had just sat down on my mat when he called and asked if I would press his legs as they were hurting. I had read that it is a great blessing to be allowed to touch the body of real saints and that as a mark of favor some saints ask their devotees to press their legs. I felt quite happy to be given this opportunity, but I kept falling asleep. Finally, it seemed as though Ratnamji was asleep so I quietly got up and went to lie down.

"Why did you stop? They still hurt," he called out.

Again I got up, this time not so eagerly. Somehow I managed to stay awake until he asked me to go and lie down. As soon as my head touched the pillow, I was fast asleep. Around 1 o'clock Ratnamji called me.

"I'm feeling cold. Is there a blanket here?"

Of course, he knew there was only one blanket, a cotton one which I was using. I covered him with it and, lying down again, I took off my dhoti and covered my body lengthwise with it. It is surprising how warm such a thin cloth could be. For a pillow I used my clothes wrapped up into a bundle or simply slept on my arm folded under my head. Though a bit uncomfortable at first I got used to it and after some time actually felt happy that I could manage with so little. It was an important step towards becoming unaffected by circumstance.

Half of our peace of mind is lost due to our reaction to circumstances, our lack of adjustability. One who wants nothing or who is ready to manage with whatever is available will be happy anywhere. Ratnamji was trying to teach me this lesson through practical experience. If he had said that one should manage with the minimum but never created such a situation, how would I have the direct knowledge or experience of it? And without practicing and experiencing it again and again, how could I understand its effect on the mind and theconsequent spiritual progress? By making me stay awake when I was ready to go to sleep, he was trying to teach me to go beyond the attachment to sleep. Also, every situation gave me an opportunity to be either selfish or selfless, as well as to develop patience and to control anger.

How many negative tendencies fill the mind can be

known only occasionally during our day to day life, but in the company of saints, whatever good or bad is within us soon comes out. It is, of course, up to the disciple to use this fact for his spiritual betterment by controlling the negative qualities and cultivating the positive ones. If, while in a sage's company, one comes to understand how one's mind works and learns how to control it, then even in the work-a-day world one will be able to live peacefully. If one survives on the battlefield, wherever he goes afterwards will be a heaven in comparison.

Getting up by 3:30 and finishing my bath, I stood ready at 4 to assist Ratnamji in any work. The previous night, in the presence of Bhaiji, I made a mild complaint that I was not getting much time for meditation nowadays. Even if I sat for meditation, I would fall asleep due to what I thought was probably exertion during the rest of the day and night. I did not know that at a certain stage of meditation the inherent dullness of the mind manifests as sleep or drowsiness. They looked at each other and then laughed. "From tomorrow you will get real meditation even without sitting for meditation," said Ratnamji. I had not understood what he meant.

Now, this morning, while washing my clothes, I felt clearly that I was an unmoving witness apart from my body and that only the body was doing the work. The feeling did not last very long. I tried to recapture it but did not succeed. My mind had felt pervaded by the same mild illumination as when I had good meditation. I asked Ratnamji about it.

"That is what I told you last night. If one repeats one's mantra always and tries to keep one's mind detached from one's work, the feeling that one is not the door starts to dawn. Of course, sitting meditation is also good, but it is only the first step. You sat for many hours every day for more than a year before coming here. That has awakened something in you. But that is only the beginning, and it will be a great limitation if you can experience that peace only when you sit down and close your eyes. That peace or current of awareness is the true nature of the mind or ego, and if you hold on to that, it will lead you to the Reality beyond the mind. If you mold your mind according to the advice of saints, that current will gain in strength and duration, becoming continuous. It will get deeper and deeper until no thought remains and you go beyond."

Ratnamji went for a bath and I followed him with a towel. He stood out by the well in the cold morning breeze drawing water and pouring it over his head again and again. I asked him why it was necessary for him to take a cold bath in the cold air at his age and stage of spirituality. He said that it was primarily to set a good example for others to follow. I asked him who are the others. I was the only person there.

"Aren't you enough? By bathing like this one becomes indifferent to the pleasures and pains of the body. Then only will it be possible to fix your mind on the internal current. Attachment to pleasure and aversion to pain are the two main obstacles to meditation. If one simply waits for pleasure and pain to come in order to practice indifference, one will have to wait a long time. The Scriptures say that we should start the day with a cold bath, preferably with well water. The dullness of sleep which pervades the nervous system will be removed, and the mind will feel fresh and alert. This, of course, does not apply to sick persons, but we are not so old or sick that we cannot observe this rule. Though it may not be strictly necessary for me, if I don't do it you will think it is not necessary for you. By not doing it, you will deprive yourself of the benefit of such a practice."

I was surprised and a bit moved at his sincerity to teach me how to purify my mind, even though it meant putting himself at an inconvenience. I knew that he had rheumatism in his knees because when they were aching I had brought hot water for him to bathe with when I was staying in the ashram. Now he disregarded his own poor health just to set an example for me to follow. I asked him why he should take this trouble for my sake.

"Do I want or expect anything from you? Of course not, but I feel that Ramana has entrusted you to my care to show you the way to Self-Realization and I know that you also feel the same. When such is the case, what is my duty? Having been entrusted with a work by one's Guru, should one not do full justice to it, even if it means suffering or even death? If complete dedication to one's God-given duty is not there, what progress one can expect either in worldly or spiritual life?

"One must control the mind and make it calm and fully concentrated in order to see the Reality shining within oneself. Total dedication to this task is necessary. One cannot go one step forward and three steps backward all the time. If we are insincere in even one action, that insincerity will become a habit and pervade all our actions. If you feel the pulse in any part of the body it will be the same.

"It is very hard to improve and mold the mind. Thus, one must be fully dedicated in whatever one does so that one's spiritual practice will be done perfectly. In fact, perfection in action is itself a most powerful practice for concentrating the mind. If I somehow can instill spirituality in you, as my Guru did for me, ceaselessly showing a good example, then if it is God's will, you will be able to do the same for someone else. Even otherwise, it will be useful for your own Liberation."

In the morning after the worship at the Samadhi, Ratnamji went to his room in the ashram in order to do his own worship. I had been picking flowers, cleaning the room, and arranging things in general, and had been attending the worship as well. Although I did not understand the principle behind it, I enjoyed the atmosphere generated by the hymns and recitation of different mantras. This morning after finishing the worship, he turned to me and asked,

"You have been sitting here for quite a few days watching the puja. When are you going to do your own?"

"Is it possible for a foreigner to do puja?" I queried. "You are repeating all of the verses in Sanskrit. If I have to learn Sanskrit, it will take a very long time indeed. Besides, I want to meditate and serve you. I don't want to spend my time learning a language."

"There is no need for you to learn Sanskrit. I myself will write out a puja in English using verses from the poetical works of Ramana and you can just learn the mechanical side of the worship and repeat the verses. It is one's devotion and intention that counts, not the language. God knows our hearts and cares little for our external actions," he replied.

So for the next couple of days, Ratnamji spent all of his

free time culling verses from Ramana's devotional poetical works and simplifying the ritual side. He explained to me the usefulness of the puja as well. He said that although ritualistic worship may be just a ritual for a priest, it is a practice for concentrating the mind for an aspirant. He gave the example of the needle on a meter. The movement at the upper end is easily visible but not so at the lower end where it is attached to the machine. Likewise, our mind is very subtle and its movements are not easily detectable. However, our actions and senses are a projection, or extension, of our mind and can be more easily watched and evaluated.

When he said this, I remembered my experience in the garden while picking flowers. I was not able to concentrate even on the flower I was picking, but was already looking for the next one. Until then I thought that I had good concentration, but in fact it was not so. He said that while doing the worship one should keep any eye out for the degree of concentration with which the mind is following the movements of the eyes and hands and hearing the verses. By improving one's concentration through the senses, one would improve power to concentrate on subtler things. Also, as concentration deepens, the screen of ignorance in the mind will gradually thin out and we will begin to see and feel the Divine Presence both within and without. When this reaches its fullest degree, that is Realization of God.

It took me nearly a month to learn the puja by heart. I took a picture of Ramana as my object of worship since, from the beginning, I had equated him with the Supreme. Obviously some force was guiding me, and I felt that force to be him. Though quite rational in everything else, in this matter I never stopped to rationalize. I intuitively felt this way, and that satisfied me sufficiently. I was seeing God in Ramana.

Too much rationalization in matters of spirituality takes the life out of it and makes one hard and dry. God being the simple, pure substratum of the mind, a childlike simplicity and faith bring one to the goal quickly. Christ also said that one must become like a child if one wants to enter the Kingdom of Heaven. To experience God, a simple childlike mind is essential. The Kingdom of Heaven is within us, but preoccupation with the waves of the mind prevents us from diving into the inner depths, to the core of our being.

Ratnamji told me that nothing fancy is needed in the way of puja materials. Simple earthenware plates would do. Some water, flowers, incense, and a piece of fruit would be enough for offering to Ramana. I started in earnest and did not miss performing the worship even for a day for the next 10 years.

Having received quite a few instructions on how to mold my every action to purify my mind, I was trying my best to put them into practice. This, however, was not an easy task. My old rebellious tendency would come up again and again. I did not have even a slight doubt about the correctness of what Ratnamji told me but when I started to do a thing, I heard two voices in my mind. "Do as he told you," "Why bother? Do as you like," said the other. For many days, I followed the second voice and did as I liked even though I knew it to be wrong.

That in itself was bad enough, but the strangest thing started to happen. Whenever I would do as I liked, I would get a knock on the head. One evening Ratnamji was sitting by the side of the pond in the ashram repeating his mantra. After two hours, he got up and started to come over to the room. At that time I was in the room trying to straighten up some things. He had kept some articles on one shelf and had told me repeatedly that I should not touch them even though they may appear to be dirty or unorganized. As I was cleaning I came to the forbidden shelf and thought, "Oh, it does not really matter if I touch the things. They are so dirty." So I started to clean and arrange the shelf. At that very moment in walked Ratnamji.

"What do you think you are doing?" he asked.

"Oh, nothing. I just thought that since I was cleaning the whole room I may as well clean here also," I replied.

"I intentionally asked you not to touch the things on that shelf as I wanted to see if you could control your impulsiveness. Obviously you cannot. How is it possible to entrust any important thing to an impulsive person? Such a one is not trustworthy. I was full of bliss and peace after repeating my mantra for two hours by the pond, and then I come here and find you doing some mischief. It is as if a huge boulder has been thrown into a calm lake," he said.

I naturally felt very bad and resolved not to go against his wishes again, but alas I repeated the same thing in different ways at least a thousand times.

One day he asked me to pluck some blades of grass to be offered in the worship. That particular type of grass only grows where there is plenty of water, and in the ashram that meant only by the side of the bathroom drain. He found that I had pulled the grass out by its roots and brought it to him. He said, "It is not necessary to kill the helpless grass. We only want the upper portion. If you just cut it with a knife then it will not die and will grow again." Easy enough, but only if one's mind goes in the right direction at the right time!

The next day when I went to pick the grass I took a knife along with me and had every intention of doing as he had told me. Just as I started to cut the grass, my mind told me, "Why listen to him? Go ahead and pull it. You can cut off the roots afterwards and he will never know." As usual, I followed the "devil's advice" and pulled the grass out by the roots. Unfortunately, I underestimated the strength of the roots and had to pull quite hard when suddenly they gave way and I went tumbling into the drainage canal! Coming out with drenched clothes, sadder but wiser, I proceeded like a criminal to Ratnamji's room fearing the trial and execution. He simply said that this is the only way I will learn, the painful way, and kept quiet.

This sort of thing started to happen day in and day out, and I was becoming frantic. It was as if I was delighting in punishing myself, or as if some unknown force was making me do the wrong thing and then enjoying the fun. Becoming confused and depressed, I began to feel that perhaps I had made a mistake by coming to spiritual life. When I thought it over, however, I could not find any preferable way of life. I had come to spiritual life not as a matter of choice borne out of logic, but rather as the result of a number of inner developments and consequent understanding of the value of spiritual life as opposed to worldly pleasures. There was simply no question of going back, or leading any other kind of life. Even if I went to go back to my previous way of life, the same understanding would assert itself and bring me back to a life of renunciation and spirituality.

Then how was I to remedy the situation? I had tried numerous times to follow the simple advice given by Ratnamji, but every time I would do just the opposite and immediately pay the price for it. I then thought that perhaps the problem was with Ratnamji. He was particular that everything should be done in a certain way. There was to be no compromising in this. Although I had accepted him as my guide, I decided I need not follow his advice. In order to escape the inevitable scolding, my mind tried to pull off a deceitful trick. I went to Ratnamji and told him that, as my company was a disturbance to him and he may lose his peace of mind, I thought it would be better if I went away.

"Where will you go?" he asked smiling all the while. He did not seem to be too upset at my proposal.

"Probably to north India," I replied.

"What will you do there?" he asked.

"Oh, probably get a Guru and do spiritual practice. Otherwise, I will get a small house in the Himalayas and spend my time growing a garden," I confidently replied.

He laughed. "God has brought you here, and without either of us searching for the other we have met and our relationship has developed. It is your time to purify the mind, and wherever you may go you will ultimately be made to do that. You are feeling that I am too strict and that if you go away you will be more peaceful, but the truth of the matter is that if you throw away what you, without asking, have been given, then you may not get it again in the near future. If you somehow do find another guide, he will be a hundred times stricter than me. When we have been brought by the Divine to spiritual life, if we run away from the little sufferings we experience in spiritual training, the Divine will give us double the suffering to make us return to the right path. Spiritual life is no joke, and if one wants to experience the Bliss of God one must first go through the pains of purification of mind and body. You need not worry about disturbing my peace of mind. It would be enough if you would persevere and try to tame your unruly mind and become peaceful yourself."

I, of course, knew that he was correct as usual, but the

same double voice continued in my mind, but perhaps a bit less after this conversation. On another day, I had been to the room of a European devotee who had lived in the ashram for many years. I had great respect for him and felt that he had certainly attained some enlightenment. He asked me how I was doing, and I told him that I felt very miserable and wished that I had never been born. He told me that as far as he could see, all my problems were due to the fact that, even though born as an American, I was trying to live like an Indian Hindu. He also said that if one listened to the Voice of God within, one could not go wrong. After speaking with him for some time I returned to my room. I thought over what he had said and decided that he must be right. I decided to go and tell Ratnamji about my new revelation and take leave of him forever. I would take the other friend's advice in the future.

I came into the room in a huff. Immediately Ratnamji said, "What is this? Sit down for some time and when you calm down we can talk. I feel as if a cyclone has entered the room!"

I told him that I had discovered the cause of all my mental agitation and also added that he should not have tried to make me into a Hindu. I recounted what my friend had said. He did not answer but got up and told me to follow him. It was night and we walked for about a mile until we reached some small hills with no people around. The moon was shining and Arunachala was shimmering in the background. Everything was silent. After sitting silently for some time, he began:

"Neal, my child, our friend is mistaken in his understanding of you. You have left America due to a Divine urge and an inborn love of India. Whatever you see or hear about in the Hindu culture makes perfect sense to you, and without anybody forcing anything on you, you have taken up the life of a traditional Hindu monk. In fact, your faith in the Vedic way of life is more than that of most orthodox Hindus. I never had any idea of making you walk in this path. I am only pointing out the way which I myself have followed. You like it and are trying to follow it. Of course, your mind rebels constantly. This is due to old deep-rooted habits you accumulated over the years before coming here. Because of the struggle between your good intentions and your past habits, you are suffering. It has nothing to do with your present way of life, although my presence no doubt is precipitating the battle. Every aspirant must eventually fight with his lower mind and come out victorious and regenerated. Though it is true that the Voice of God is within us, there are many other voices within us as well. Of those, the subtlest is God's, and in your present state you cannot possibly differentiate properly which is His and which is the "devils," so to speak. Until you gain enough mental purity to do so, the safe course is to trust your teacher and follow his advice, however trying it may be. I want only your betterment and have no desire to cause you any suffering. Try to understand the depth of my affection for you, spiritual as it is, and taking confidence in that, go on trying to purify your mind. At present, the little light that you have is mixed with much darkness. That has to be recognized and removed. Do not worry so much. Ramana has brought you this far and will show you the rest of the way."

These soothing words were a balm to my soul, but within a few days I again started to suffer due to the conflicting voices in my mind. I thought that it was a hopeless cause to make my mind pure and actually contemplated suicide, though I probably did not have the courage to do such a thing. At that time, I came across a conversation between Ramana and a devotee concerning suicide. Ramana told the devotee that suicide is spiritually as bad for oneself as murder. Though pain may be due to the body, suffering is of the mind, and it is the mind that must be killed, not the innocent body. One who kills his own body must still complete the suffering of his present birth after death, with the additional sufferings brought about by the sin of suicide. Instead of suicide being a solution, suicide only worsens matters. A person who has committed suicide can never attain peace of mind after death.

This, of course, precluded the possibility of suicide for me. There was simply no choice but to forge ahead and continue to try to make the mind obey my will. I wished so much that I could be in harmony with Ratnamji and that he would not have to correct me and scold me constantly. It was certainly no pleasure for him, and it was hell for me. Though I would have gladly run away any number of times, there was always something deep within me that said, "Everything is happening for the best. Do not give up, but go bravely through this dark night of the soul." I had not even read about the dark night of the soul, but I was certainly in the midst of it. This painful condition lasted for nearly one year, while I was learning and struggling to apply what I was taught by Ratnamji.

At the end of one year, Ratnamji asked me to invite my mother to India. He told me that I had left her in a very callous way. In fact, I had treated her with disrespect and disregard most of my life due to the usual selfishness and arrogance common to children. Unlike the culture of India, American culture does not stress the fact that one should, as much as possible, obey one's parents. Cherishing them, one should pay back the debt owed to them for having raised and provided for oneself. Either as a matter of duty or out of love, one should look after one's parents and maintain good relations with them. Without the blessings of one's mother, no real progress is possible in spiritual life. This is the opinion of the ancient sages. It is told in the Scriptures that an ungrateful person cannot even find a place in hell. However, if one's parents give advice or request one to do something which is harmful for one's spiritual life, one need not obey them. Only words of one's spiritual guide hold more weight than those of one's parents.

I wrote to my mother and she agreed to come as soon as possible, along with my sister. At that juncture, Ratnamji told me that he was going to Hyderabad to visit some devotees and relatives who were eager to see him after a long time. He told me that if I liked I could bring my mother there or, after her return to America, I should come there alone to meet other devotees and saints. On the way to the bus stand, he told me I should try to see Ramana in my mother and serve her as such. This would please God, and my mother also would be pleased, though not knowing why. A devotee of God must love God alone, but when he does so all creation receives his love, as God resides in the hearts of all. With these words, he got into the bus and was gone. I was left to myself, awaiting a new chapter in my life.

Ratnamji

Chapter 3

PROGRESSION

After a few days, my mother and sister arrived by car from Madras. I had them accommodated in the ashram guest house. My mother was overjoyed to see me after more than a year of separation. She was surprised to see that I had cut my long hair, shaved my beard, and was wearing only a dhoti and a towel. I prostrated to her as enjoined by the Hindu scriptures.

"What is this?" she exclaimed. "Why are you lying down on the ground in front of me?"

"Mother, I am not lying down. I am prostrating before you in order to get your blessing," I calmly replied.

"If you want my blessing, please do not do such a thing again. Who ever heard of such a thing? I do not like it," she said, a bit pained to see her son humiliating himself before her.

"Mother, please bear with me. Of course you do not like it, but I must get the right attitude of seeing God in you. You know, when Moses saw God in the burning bush on Mount Sinai, he fell on the ground like a log of wood due to devotion and reverence. By practicing like this, I will eventually be able to see God in everyone and everything," I tried to explain to her.

"Well, you can do it to others if you wish. Don't do it to me!" she retorted.

After making them comfortable, I took them to my little room where I had been staying for nearly a year. She was somewhat pained to see the simplicity of my life style. When at home, I had used a one foot thick mattress and foam pillows, while here I was laying on a mat without even a sheet or pillow. I told her about my daily routine of getting up at 3:30 in the morning and going to bed around 11 at night. I also showed her my puja, or worship. I even tried to cook something for her, but it was so bad even a cow could not have eaten it.

Even then, with her usual patience, she appreciated everything and encouraged me to continue in my chosen path, although it would have made her much happier to see me lead a more normal life. Unfortunately, after a few days she came down with dysentery and had to spend the remaining days in bed. I took it as God's will to give me a chance to serve her and tried my best to nurse her back to health. After an uneventful stay of two weeks, my sister and I took mother to Madras for the return trip home. My sister decided to return to Tiruvannamalai. She stayed there for the next six months, meditating and studying.

I took the first available train to Hyderabad and reached there the next morning. On the way I noticed a vast change in my mental state. The usual confusion and struggle in my mind had given way to a current of peace. I had felt this current now and then, but now it persisted for longer periods in the morning before sunrise and in the evening after sunset. It occurred spontaneously without my meditating. Even at other times during the day I felt more peaceful and happy. Was it the result of obeying Ratnamji and receiving the blessing of my mother? I was confident that I would be in greater harmony with him when I saw him again.

After reaching Hyderabad, I located the house at which Ratnamji was supposed to be staying but learned he was in the hospital.

"What do you mean in the hospital? I think you are referring to a different person." I thought perhaps I had come to the wrong house.

"No, Ratnamji is my younger brother. He told me that you would be coming. I am sorry to say that he is in the hospital with a fractured hip."

I could not believe what I was hearing. How could such a saintly person be involved in such an accident? I was, of course, very naive at that time and thought that saints are never put through the hardships of life like ordinary people. During the next seven years with Ratnamji, I was to see that saints actually are made to suffer much more than the common man.

"Come in. After lunch I will take you there," his brother

assured me. He was an elderly man of about sixty-five, a retired railway official. He had a motherly concern for Ratnamji. He sent a little money to him every month so that he would not suffer from lack of food. Ratnamji took this as a Divine dispensation. Whenever he would come to Hyderabad, he would spend some days at his brother's house trying to instill some spiritual ideas into him.

"How did he break his hip?" I asked, after washing up and taking a seat in the parlour.

"He was attending a bhajan (a gathering where devotional songs are sung) at a friend's house. The next morning he was supposed to come here, as we were going to perform the annual ceremony for our departed parents. His friend's son offered to bring him here on a motor scooter, and Ratnamji agreed. As they were making a turn, a taxi hit them from the side and knocked him off. The driver was unhurt, but due to the force of the fall, Ratnamji broke his hip. That was two days ago. They have still not set the bone, as it requires an operation. He is diabetic. The doctor wants to bring his blood sugar count down to normal before doing anything," his brother replied.

After lunch, we took a bus to the hospital. It was about five miles away, and I got a chance to see a bit of the city. The bus was a double-decker type like those in London, and so we sat on the upper deck in order to have a better view of the town. Hyderabad is one of the most beautiful cities in India. It has wide thoroughfares with plenty of shady trees growing along both sides of the roads. There are many parks and a great deal of open space, with a small river meandering through the heart of the city. The Moghul influence is seen everywhere in the city's architecture. It is actually a twin city, Secunderabad being the sister city. The people are very polite and courteous. Because the city is located near the center of India, many saints of all religions pass through there, and one can always find some devotional program going on somewhere in the city.

We reached the huge government hospital, and going up to the second floor, came to the men's surgical ward. There were about a hundred patients in the ward. His brother took me over to a bed where Ratnamji was lying with a big smile beaming on his face!

"This is terrible! How could such an accident happen to you?" I exclaimed with tears in my eyes, even without greeting him.

"Accident? Is there such a thing? Is birth an accident? Is death an accident? It is all Ramana's sweet will for my spiritual good. For a devotee of God, there is no such thing as fate or accidents. Whatever happens to him is happening by the gracious will of his Beloved God, Who is ever busy trying to take the devotee back to Himself. We should be happy in whatever situation He places us," Ratnamji replied, smiling.

He certainly practiced what he preached. He seemed to be as happy as ever though tied to a bed unable to move this way or that. The doctor had put a temporary frame on his leg to prevent any movement of the leg. It was obviously very uncomfortable.

"How did you know that I was here?" Ratnamji questioned me.

"I did not suspect that you were in a hospital. After my mother left, I took the next train. When I reached Hyderabad, I went directly to your brother's house whose address I got from your letter file. I was shocked to hear about your accident and thought that I was in the wrong house, but now I see that it is so," I replied almost in tears, seeing him on the bed like that. He had always been so active, and now he was confined like a prisoner.

He affectionately touched my arm. Trying to comfort me, he said, "Don't be so upset. Some good will certainly come out of this. Everyone was worried that there would be no one to look after me here. They are all having to attend to their offices, schools, and families. Who is going to look after a poor monk? Nobody expressed it in so many words, but I could understand what was going on in their minds. I told my brother this morning, 'I have offered everything to Ramana. He will look after me, you will see.' Now you have come here, just at the right time. These friends and relatives were coming here in shifts to serve me, but they were feeling a little inconvenienced. Well, who sent Neal here just at this time? Was it not Ramana? The worldly people have faith only in the world. God is an abstract, hazy idea for them. For us, it is just the opposite. He alone is real, and this world is a hazy dream in comparison."

Someone asked me how long I would be staying in Hyderabad. Actually, a selfish idea was going through my mind. I thought that I would spend a few days making Ratnamji comfortable and then go back to the peace of the ashram. I was apprehensive that his company would again start a turmoil in my mind.

"He'll go only after I can walk again by myself," Ratnamji answered even before I could open my mouth. At the moment of hearing these words, I also felt in my heart of hearts that it would be very wrong to leave him here like this, and took his pronouncement as the Divine command.

The coming days saw a continuous flow of visitors to Ratnamji's bedside. He had been raised and educated in Hyderabad and had visited many times after the demise of Ramana. Whoever heard about the accident came to the hospital. Even after the hospital closed its gates to visitors at night, the resident physicians and medical officers came in to meet him and hear spiritual talk from his lips. One devotee gave me a blanket and, with the permission of the hospital superintendent, I slept on the floor near his bed at night and attended him during the day. Although the hospital supplied food for him, some devotees from the outside brought food for me every day. We kept a picture of Ramana on the nightstand beside his bed, and I picked a few flowers from the garden every day and decorated it. After making him comfortable in the morning, I went for my bath in the house of a devotee who lived nearby and, finishing my daily worship or puja, returned within two hours. This was the only time of the day that I left the hospital after making sure that Ratnamji would need nothing immediately.

Within one week his diabetic condition had improved enough to allow the doctors to operate. On the day of the operation, about 40 people came in the morning to be with him. I was just thinking about Bhaiji, wondering whether he would come, when at that very moment he walked into the ward. I mentioned to Ratnamji about this coincidence. He told me, "Even if such things happen, one should not feel any exhilaration about it. Even if psychic powers come to us we should not accept them, for we will be deflected from our path of realizing God. Before the Bliss of God Realization, all supernatural powers are as dust."

Bhaiji, in his usual jolly mood, sat down next to the bed. After inquiring about his health and the coming operation, he started to sing the Name of God along with Ratnamji. What followed is difficult to describe in words.

A nurse came and started to rub the fractured place with alcohol in order to clean it in preparation for the operation. The pain was excruciating and Ratnamji started to sing the Divine Name louder. Suddenly he started to laugh uproariously. The next moment his eyes became fixed, his breath stopped, his chest flushed and all of the hair on his head and body stood out like porcupine quills, as if an electric current was passing through him. As I watched with wonder I saw that his eyes gradually changed from brown to a brilliant blue-white, the color of an arc lamp or a welding gun. Was this Samadhi, the Supreme Bliss of union with God?

After a few moments his body relaxed a bit, and in a choked voice he laughed and talked excitedly about the Ocean of Power which is God. Before he could say the word God, his mind soared up again into the Light, and all his hairs stood on end as before. This happened a number of times. A moment later, the doctor came to the bedside to see if he was ready for the operation. The doctor's name was Rama which is a name of God in the Sanskrit language. One look at the doctor and Ratnamji was gone, back to the Abode of Infinite Bliss. Coming down, he stammered, "Rama, Rama, even the thought of Your Name is making me like this!" The doctor and nurse, of course, could not make head nor tail of what he meant. They thought that he was hysterical from fear of the impending operation. They told him not to worry, that he would be put under anesthesia and would not feel anything.

"I am not worried. To tell you the truth, anesthesia is not at all necessary. Even if you don't use it I wouldn't feel the slightest pain!" he exclaimed laughing.

Not grasping the significance of what he was saying, they again reassured him and told him to get ready. In a few minutes, they would wheel him to the operation theater. Seeing this wonderful state of his and having read of such things in books describing the lives of Realized Souls, I was fondly wishing in my mind that I could have such an experience of union with the Supreme Light as I had just witnessed. Just as I finished thinking the above, Ratnamji turned to me and said, "Is it possible so soon? First you must practice and become ripe, and then it will come." Obviously my mind was an open book to him.

After he came back from the operating room, some devotees sat near his bed. The peace radiating from him was tremendous. My thought waves more or less subsided, and I was enjoying a deep peace like dreamless sleep. Gradually, he became conscious as the effect of the anesthesia wore off, and he laughed and joked with everyone until late in the night. The doctors had put a steel rod through his shin bone below the knee in order to pull the leg in traction. I felt much pain to see that.

Due to the neglect of the doctors, the wound around the rod became septic during the next few days, and caused him unbearable agony. He could not move and was extremely restless due to the pain. The doctors were told of the infection and asked to clean the wound and administer antibiotics. However, they forgot and delayed for nearly four or five days.

Finally, one night a young man who was studying for his medical degree came to talk to Ratnamji. I told him about the septic condition of the wound, and he immediately cleaned it and administered some medicines. After that, he came every day to talk to Ratnamji and to clean the wound himself. I was surprised and angry at the callousness of the hospital staff and decided then and there that it would be better to die in a gutter unattended than to die in a hospital in the hands of such indifferent people.

In the coming years, I had many opportunities to visit hospitals, and always it was the same. The attending nurses and doctors seemed to forget that inside the human body there are nerves, and connected to the nerves is a person who can clearly feel pain. Practice of the healing art is indeed an opportunity to either selflessly serve one's fellow man and learn to see God in him or to act as a messenger of the god of death, to torture others. As for the patient, being in a hospital is a good chance to practice utter surrender to

God's will.

For nearly two months Ratnamji was kept in traction. After taking X-rays, the doctors learned that, due to his diabetic condition, the fracture was healing very slowly. They decided to remove the rod from his leg and attach the traction by means of adhesive plaster wrapped around his leg. Though this was more comfortable initially, Ratnamji started to complain after a few days that it felt as if the skin on his leg was being torn off. The doctors, of course, did not believe him and insisted that the feeling was only in his imagination. He suffered this torture for another month, when the plaster was finally removed. All of the skin under the plaster had indeed been slowly torn off by the weight of the traction. The scars from this could be seen on his leg for years afterwards. I asked him why he was having to suffer so much.

"Each one has done virtuous as well as wicked deeds during the course of numberless lives. As one sows, so must one reap. Whatever comes to us unasked is only the fruit of our own deeds. Virtuous actions yield pleasant fruit; evil deeds yield painful fruit. Reaping the fruits may not, and usually does not, happen in the same birth as the actions. God arranges the fruits of our deeds in such a way as to take us gradually to higher and higher planes of spiritual realization. It is up to us to use His dispensation to make progress spiritually. By remaining as an unmoved witness to the pleasures and pains of the body, one's mind gradually becomes pure and merges into its source, which is God or the Real Self of all. One can be overjoyed at the pleasant and miserable about the painful, as indeed most people do, but this won't take one any closer to the goal of even-mindedness.

All my pains are the fruits of some wicked deeds I did at some time in the past. The sufferings coming now are serving to push my mind up into sublime heights of God-consciousness. Why should I complain or blame others? Though the fruit of a wicked deed, God is using it to give me His Vision. What a wonder!" he replied.

One day a devotee came in the evening to see Ratnamji. He was married, with three children, and had a small herbal shop. He sat down by the side of the bed on the floor and started to repeat the Divine Name softly. I was sitting beside him, watching him. I had the idea in my mind that married people could not make much progress spiritually due to the fact that most of their energy and time must go to their families. Gary in Japan was an exception, but even he had first gone through many years of strict discipline as a monk. This man was deeply immersed in singing the Name of God when suddenly a heavy book, which was sitting on the bed, crashed down on some plates just next to him. Startled, I jumped but he did not even flinch or open his eyes. He just kept up his singing as if nothing had happened. Ratnamji looked at me with a smile in his eyes.

"If one can repeat the Divine Name with such absorption that there is no awareness of one's body or surroundings," he said. "What does it matter if one is married or has children? This man's whole mind is given over to God. Every minute of the day he is repeating the Divine Name within, even though he has to attend to his business and family. He has no attachment to anyone or anything but goes along doing his duty in a detached spirit as an offering to God. Thinking of the Supreme all of the time and seeking the company of saints whenever time permits, his mind easily loses itself in meditation when he sits for repeating the Name. Who is better, him or us? Though monks, do we have this kind of absorption?"

This taught me that one should not judge a man's spiritual stature by his station in life. An all-renouncing monk may be as shallow as a puddle of water, and a householder may be as deep as the ocean in spiritual achievement.

It was during Ratnamji's stay in the hospital that I came to meet the great saint Avadbutendra Swamiji. He and Ratnamji had been close friends for about 20 years and had traveled together all over India. Swamiji was an excellent musician and spent two hours every night singing the Divine Name in private houses or at religious centers. His singing had a quality about it which would cause the air to become electrified with devotion. I asked him if he would tell me a little about his past so that I might gain some inspiration to increase my own efforts at God Realization.

He told me that he had studied music in North India for a year, at which time his teacher told him that there was nothing more to teach him, he had an inborn genius for music. Some film producers asked him to sing the sound tracks for their films, but he declined saying that God had given him his voice and he would use it only for Him. He then went further north to Ayodhya, the birth place of Sri Rama, considered in India to have been a Divine Incarnation of ancient times, where he joined an ashram.

As the days went by and he was engaged in his spiritual disciplines and practices, he found that paralysis was gradually overtaking his body. He consulted many doctors and tried many medicines but to no avail. Finally, the paralysis was so great that he could not speak. He expected to die within a short time. At that time, a fellow monk showed him a little booklet entitled Hanuman Chalisa, which was a composition by a saint named Tulasidas who had lived about 400 years ago. It was comprised of 40 verses in praise of Hanuman, Sri Rama's closest devotee and servant. He told Swamiji that he should try to repeat the verses mentally as best he could because many people had been cured of incurable diseases by doing so. Swamiji somehow managed to memorize the verses and went on repeating the hymn. To his surprise, his voice gradually came back and the paralysis completely vanished within a month after he started the repetition.

Swamji decided to show his gratitude to Hanuman in a concrete way. During the next 40 years he made it a point to get this hymn engraved in marble and installed in every Hanuman temple he could find in North and Central India. This was about 200 temples! He told me that various devotees had offered to bear the cost of doing this, and even when he received money for his own use he would use it for this purpose.

After being cured he went in search of a realized Guru and found one in a small town near where the Yamuna and Ganges rivers meet. This saint, Prabhudattaji, had been doing penance under a tree for many years and had attained Illumination. He was well known in these parts. Swamiji approached him but was put to a severe test before being accepted as a disciple.

Prabhudattaji gave Swamiji a job watering a garden of basil plants which are considered to be a very holy plant in

India. The garden was so large that it required about 100 buckets of water every day. A well was nearby, but it was more than a hundred feet deep. On top of this, it was the cold season and Swamiji's hands started to crack while drawing the water. After a few days his hands were covered with blood, but he wrapped them in a piece of rug and continued doing the work without a murmur. After a month his Guru gave him another job. He was to clean all of the cooking pots in the ashram every day. Prabhudattaji's ashram is a very big one, and hundreds of people are fed there daily. Swamiji said that the pots were so big he would have to sit inside them in order to clean them!

After he did this job for some days, his Guru felt that he had passed the test, and took him into his personal service for the next 15 years. He also asked him to sing the Divine Name in the ashram every night. Swamiji would become so overpowered with Divine Love while singing that on many days he could not continue the songs. Seeing this, his Guru called him one day and told him that he was ready to be on his own and was free to go. This was after serving his Guru for 15 years.

From that time onwards, he wandered all over the country singing the Divine Name and preaching Its greatness as a means of realizing God. He told me that in all the 40 years of his wandering from holy place to holy place, he had never met a saint as great as Ratnamji and always found Supreme Bliss in his company. Hearing that Ratnamji was in the hospital, he had come from a far away town just to see him.

Swamiji was a majestic figure. If you did not know he was a monk you would think he was a king. He was six feet tall with long arms and a deep voice. His eyes had the softness of a doe and his face was ever lit with a smile. I felt privileged to meet him. Now and then, Ratnamji would send me to attend his singing so I could get better acquainted with him. He always asked me to sit next to him and treated me with great kindness and even respect. This always made me feel uneasy, but he was teaching us all how we should treat devotees of God as being God Himself. If we could do this, it would be just one more step toward seeing God in all.

Ratnamji had been in the hospital for four months when I began to feel impatient to get out of there, but he kept telling me to surrender to Ramana's will. I was amazed at his patience. I could at least walk wherever I liked, but he was confined to the bed, yet he did not seem the least bit impatient. Finally, on waking one morning, I felt a distinct difference in the atmosphere, a kind of peace or lightness. Perhaps it was only my imagination.

Whatever it might have been, that morning the doctors told us that Ratnamji could leave the hospital that day. Oh joy! But my joy did not last long. Ratnamji asked the doctors if they were sure it was all right to go. I was shocked to hear him say this. What if they should change their minds, I thought. Even mindedness in pleasure and pain—there was little of that quality in me, and there was little of anything else in Ratnamji! The doctors reassured him that he could go but that he should not try to walk for another month. Thank God, we would be going after all. We carried Ratnamji to a taxi and drove to the house of a friend who had invited him to convalesce there as long as necessary. On the way I asked Ratnamji, "How does the sky look after so many months indoors?"

"It looks just like the ceiling of the hospital ward!" he replied, laughing. His equal vision was indeed incorrigible.

Any place Ratnamji stayed became an ashram within a few days, and our new residence was no exception. Our friend was a government official and the government had given him a sprawling mansion as residential quarters. It was situated in a large garden of about four or five acres in the suburban area of Hyderabad. What a relief after the depressing atmosphere of the hospital! Being in the hospital no doubt had its valuable lessons. Every day one saw one or two patients die right in front of one's eyes, and the true nature of the human body became grossly obvious. But for all that, I would not like to spend the rest of my life there!

Our friend was a devotee of a famous Indian saint. Every week he would hold meetings and give discourses on the teachings of his Guru and also hold meditation classes. He had great respect for Ratnamji and really felt it a privilege to serve him in his house. They spent hours together discussing spiritual topics late into the night. During the day, while he was at his office, other devotees came to visit Ratnamji for devotional singing, worship, or discussions. There was never a dull moment in Ratnamji's company.

My routine did not change. I arose at 3:30, bathed and conducted puja. I then attended to Ratnamji's needs— bathing him, washing his clothes, cleaning the room, writing his letters, and any other necessary work. There was always something to do. He once told me that a lazy man can never find anything to do, and a sincere man can never find any leisure. I wanted to be the latter, so I always kept myself busy. If there was no work and my scriptural studies had been done, he asked me to help the house people or the servants with their work. After all, we were guests in their house, and we should share the work. That was his attitude, and even he did whatever he could to help the host and his family.

Many times, when we stayed with poor families during our travels, he asked me to purchase food and give it to whoever was cooking. When leaving, we sometimes arranged for money to be given to them after our departure, as they might hesitate to take it from us directly. If the hosts were wealthy, we at least offered our physical services. In the government official's house, I was doing this, but usually without their knowing lest they feel upset. Ratnamji felt that even if others show respect to us, we should never feel that we are in any way better than them, but rather we must cultivate a feeling of oneness and equality with all.

One morning after bathing, I was about to sit down to do my daily worship when Ratnamji called me.

"I want to see your puja today. Do it near my bed. I have not seen how you do it for many months," he said.

I arranged everything near his bed and started the puja. I did the worship for about five minutes, then he asked me to stop.

"You are repeating the verses mechanically, without any feeling. Not only that, you are offering something to your Guru without even looking at him. If I should offer you a glass of water and, while putting it in your hands, turn towards the window and say, 'Please accept this,' how would you feel? If you do the puja correctly, your concentration will deepen day by day, and you will start to feel that the image or photo is alive. Try to do it as I have told you," he instructed.

I started from the beginning and tried to do as he said. While offering some flowers to Ramana's photo, I looked directly at him and then placed them at his feet. As I did this I was surprised at the feeling of love towards him that I felt in my heart. At the same time, my eyes became slightly closed and tears started to come of their own accord. Not only that, I clearly saw a living quality in the photo. I was surprised at the accuracy of Ratnamji's diagnosis and felt badly that I had let so many days slip by without doing the puja properly and getting the benefit and Bliss from it. I resolved to ask him now and then if I was doing my spiritual practices properly.

One morning, I went out in the garden to pick flowers for the worship. As I passed under a tree, I clearly saw and heard all of the leaves tremble. I thought it must be the wind blowing the leaves, but there was scarcely any wind, certainly not enough to make all of the leaves flutter. I became curious and walked under the tree again. Again the leaves trembled. I tried this a number of times with almost the same result and then went running into the house to tell Ratnamji about it.

"What is the wonder in it? Trees are living beings just like us. They have their own feelings and sensations. However, you should not dwell on it, or else you will forget what you are staying here for. Even an unusual happening should not distract our attention. I noticed the other day when I called you in from outside that you looked to and fro at the monkeys playing in the trees. A spiritual aspirant should be so intent on his aim that, unless necessary, he never gets distracted by anything.

"There is a story that Sri Rama asked Hanuman to jump across a large body of water to get some information from the other side. While he was leaping across, some aquatic creatures offered their backs for him to rest on, but he declined and went straight ahead and finished the work. We should also be like that and not let anything distract us," he replied.

He was, of course, right as usual, but for some reason I

felt a bit hurt at his words. After giving me this advice, he asked me to go down the road about 1/4 mile to another devotee's house and tell him to come as soon as possible. I felt rebellious, and said that I would do it later. He insisted that it should be done at once. I felt a little angry at his insistence, and instead of obeying him, I went into the bathroom and took a cold shower. I was surprised to find that after finishing my shower, my rebellious mood and anger had vanished. I went to him and apologized and then told him what had happened.

"Sometimes due to heated nerves a person will be irritable or angry. Taking a cold shower cools the nerves, and the anger subsides. The feeling of lust is similar. In fact, all passions heat up the nerves or may be aroused due to heated nerves. A cold shower is a good remedy," he said.

After a month, Ratnamji started to walk. Within two months, he could walk quite well with the help of a stick. He called me one day and told me,

"Once, about 26 years ago when I was serving Ramana, he had asked a visiting devotee whether he had ever been to a holy place called Muktinath in Nepal. It is the place from which the holy saligram stone comes from. This stone is found in abundance in the Gandaki River, which flows by that place, and is used in India for purposes of worship. Ever since hearing about the place, I had wanted to visit there, as it is considered to be one of the most ancient places of pilgrimage.

"It is said in the Scriptures that a king named Bharata, after leaving his kingdom in the care of his sons, retired to Muktinath to do penance. He did indeed reach a high spiritual state, but because he developed a strong attachment for a young deer, he died thinking only of the deer instead of the Supreme Truth. As a result, he was reborn as a deer. "The Scriptures aver that one's next birth is largely determined by the nature of one's last thought while dying. For this reason, the Divine Name is loudly chanted near a dying man. If he can think of God at that moment, he will merge in Him and attain the highest Bliss.

"The other day, Swamiji asked me if I would like to accompany him to Nepal. Two other people will be coming. If we decide to go, I will ask my oldest sister to come along with us to do the cooking. She has accompanied me on various pilgrimages over the years and likes it very much. What do you say?"

I was naturally very eager to go, especially in the company of two saints. I gladly agreed and Swamiji was informed. We were to start after one week and would visit other places on the way. Ratnamji's sister arrived within a few days. We got everything ready and went to meet Swamiji.

Our party of six was met at the train station by a large group of devotees who had come to see the two saints off. It was a joy to be with even one of them; one can well imagine the happiness of being with both of them at once! Ratnamji and Swamiji were both at their best when in each other's company, and I felt a great happiness at seeing them together. One was a great singer of devotional songs, and the other could raise one's level of consciousness through his words of wisdom. Both of them had renounced all worldly interests in order to attain God Realization and had achieved much in the spiritual world. In addition, they were both like children, simple and innocent without a bit of false pride or arrogance in them.

We spent the next 10 days traveling towards Nepal, stopping at holy places along the way, visiting temples, and staying with Swamiji's devotees. During his 40 years of traveling around the country, Swamiji had gained quite a few admirers and he usually knew at least one person in each town we stopped in.

Traveling in the company of two saints, one had no time to think of anything other than God. I had come to India not even believing or caring whether there was a God. Now I found that my mind was full of the thought of Him alone. How had that happened? It was certainly due to being in the company of saints. The feverishness and insipidness of worldly life had been replaced by a continuous feeling of inner peace and Bliss. Every moment held a fascination of its own. The current of peace and light was increasing day by day, holding the promise of Oneness at the end.

The goal of my life was the highest that man could aspire for, identity with his Creator and the Infinite Bliss and knowledge that goes with it. I had somehow managed to come into intimate contact with a tradition which had been followed, tested, and proved over thousands of years to promote spiritual evolution. I was now living in the company and under the guidance of two sages who were witnesses to the grandeur and Truth of the ancient traditions. Thinking like this, tears welled up in my eyes. I felt that I was a nobody and a nothing, being blown like a dry leaf by the favorable wind of the Divine will.

Swamiji rarely gave me any instructions. Although I sometimes washed his clothes and carried his luggage, he felt that I was Ratnamji's spiritual son and there was no need for him to instruct me. Only on one occasion did I receive advice from him. One day, as we walked through the streets on our way to a temple, a man accosted me and asked me from which country I hailed. I started to answer him when Swamiji turned around and asked what I was talking about. I told him about the man's question. He replied,

"If one repeats the Divine Name with every breath then one can achieve God-consciousness very soon. People don't succeed because they waste much time in unnecessary talk. In the amount of time that it takes you to listen to and answer this man's question, you could repeat your mantra at least 10 times. Is that not a great loss?"

We traveled further north and at last came to the Nepal border. From there, one can either take a very tedious bus journey or a plane to reach Kathmandu, the capital of Nepal. Ratnamji advised me to look after all of Swamiji's expenses as well as the expenses for the three of us. I decided that we should go by plane regardless of the cost. It would be more comfortable for them and, as Ratnamji had never been in a plane, I wanted him to have the experience at least once. We got into the plane and were soon flying over the Himalayas. Ratnamji was just like a child and eagerly looked out the window at the ground far below. He said to me,

"You know, this is very similar to God-consciousness. As the mind soars higher and higher towards its Source, the sense of differentiation is gradually lost until at last everything is merged into the One Existence. As we fly higher and higher, the objects below are losing their relative sizes. People, trees, buildings, and even hills all appear to be the same height. If we were to go high enough, the earth itself would disappear in the vastness of space!"

I was surprised at the way he looked at things. His mind was always tuned to God no matter what might be happening.

On arriving in Kathmandu, we went by car to an inn near the main temple of the city, Pasupathinath. The inn was a rest house for pilgrims visiting the temple. It was a two-story building, the ground floor being used to keep cows and the upper floor for guests. It was free, but one could make a donation. We took a room, spread out our bedding, and took a little rest before proceeding to the temple.

The Pasupathinath Temple is a huge complex within a compound wall and, although Hindu, the architectural style, pagoda-shaped, is Far Eastern. Hundreds of devotees go in and out of the temple from early morning until late at night. The climate in the Kathmandu Valley is very cool and refreshing. I felt as if a great weight had been lifted off my shoulders after leaving the heat of the Indian plains. Ratnamji and Swamiji also liked the place immensely and were like two small children, looking at everything and enjoying the new surroundings and culture.

The next day we took a taxi and went to all of the important sights in the city, among which were many Hindu and Buddhist temples. We then went to one of the neighboring villages, where there was a famous and ancient temple dedicated to the Divine Mother. A few yards away from the temple, we heard loud devotional singing. Swamiji, being attracted to that and curious to see what was going on, led us into a huge courtyard. Hundreds of people were chanting the Divine Name to the accompaniment of drums and harmoniums. In the center of the crowd was an elderly gentleman, swaying to the music and throwing flowers on everyone near him. He had a radiant countenance. On seeing Swamiji, he jumped up, came over to him, and embraced him.

Swamiji was very happy and told us that this gentleman was one of the greatest saints of Nepal. He was spending his whole life spreading the Divine Name across Nepal and northern India. Swamiji had met him before in India where this saint had an ashram in Brindavan, a holy place associated with the life and past times of Sri Krishna, an Incarnation of the Supreme Being. Swamiji and Gautamji, as he was called, were surprised and overjoyed at this chance meeting. We were invited in and fed sumptuously. At night, we returned to our inn promising to go to Gautamji's Kathmandu ashram which was just a five-minute walk from where we were staying.

The next day, the six of us went to the ashram, which was on a hill between the temple and our inn. It was actually the ancestral house of Gautamji's family. When we arrived, a festival was in full swing. Gautamji's son was dressed as Sri Krishna, and some of the devotees were dressed as His companions. They performed gymnastic feats and games, as cowherd children do when they take the cows to pasture and play in the fields—as Sri Krishna had done as a child. All the while, loud chanting of the Divine Name was going on. The atmosphere was charged with devotion. After the performance, food was distributed to everyone.

Gautamji then took us out into the garden to show us the rest of the ashram. The garden contained two small temples and a number of stone pillars. The temples contained the Holy Scriptures of the Hindus including the four Vedas, *Mahabharata*, *Ramayana* and the 18 Mahapuranas. The Hindu culture has a vast treasure of religious literature to help all people at any stage of spiritual evolution. As in any other religion, the Scriptures are revered and worshipped as the revealed Word of God.

We asked Gautamji about the stone pillars. He told us that, over the years, he had advised his devotees to repeat the Name of God continuously and also to write It down in notebooks. He had collected a vast number of such notebooks with the Divine Name "Rama" written in them. He had buried them in the ground and installed pillars over them to mark the spots. The pillars were offerings of visible representations of the Divine Name. We asked him how many Names had been buried under the five or six pillars in the garden. He told us that under each pillar "Rama" was written in the notebooks million of times! We were speechless with wonder. We had never seen such devotion to the

Divine Name anywhere.

Gautamji then drove us to a small village about 20 miles from Kathmandu where he had another ashram. The lush green of the countryside, with the Himalayas in the distance, was a beautiful sight for all of us. The Nepali villagers are perhaps the most cultured, religious, and simple people in the world. I felt that perhaps the Indian people had been like them a thousand years ago before the Mogul and British invasions spoiled the ancient culture's pristine purity.

When we reached the village ashram, we were escorted by one of the residents. He showed us a small artificial hill in the center of the ashram, which had been made out of cement or plaster of paris. We were told that some stones had been brought from the holy Govardhana Mountain in India. This mountain was associated with Sri Krishna. The stones had been placed in the center of the ashram, and a replica of the Govardhana Hill was built over them. As is done at Govardhana, the devotees walked around the miniature hill, singing and chanting the Names and stories of Lord Krishna.

In another spot was an area about seven by three feet with a pillar in each corner. We were told that, just like the pillars in the Kathmandu ashram, this open space contained another 10 million Names. When anyone in the surrounding area was dying, his body was brought here and placed on this spot. The people felt that the spiritual vibrations of the Name would be of immense help to the departing soul. Swamiji, who had been repeating the Divine Name for 40 years and propagating It all over India was surprised and overjoyed at this childlike faith in God and His Name. In fact, standing on that spot, he had no inclination to return to India. He turned to us and said,

"These simple folk have full devotion to God. In India we cannot find people with even one-tenth this much faith. I do not feel like returning there!"

It was September, and the weather in the Kathmandu Valley was very chilly in the early morning. Swamiji had not been in good health for some time, and he felt uncomfortable due to the cold. He finally decided to return to India with the other two devotees as soon as possible. We discussed our future plans, and Ratnamji instructed me to purchase a plane ticket to India for Swamiji and to get three tickets for us to Pokhara, a village about 400 miles to the west of Kathmandu. It was from there that we would have to start our pilgrimage to Muktinath. Swamiji's flight was available the next day, but seats to Pokhara were available only after three days. After booking everything I returned to the inn.

The next morning when Ratnamji woke up, he was burning with high fever. He could hardly stand up. Swamiji wanted to go to the temple before returning to India, and Ratnamji insisted on accompanying him. He supported himself on my shoulder, and we slowly made our way to the temple and back. As soon as we reached the inn, Ratnamji became unconscious. Swamiji and I put him into a taxi and went to a homeopathic doctor, purchased medicines, and returned.

Swamiji's plane was scheduled to depart at 11:00 a.m. It was already 9 o'clock. How could he leave Ratnamji in this condition? He asked me again and again if he should go. I assured him that Ratnamji's sister and I would look after everything and asked him not to worry. Finally, giving me his costly woolen blanket for Ratnamji, he bade us farewell with a sad look on his face.

Ratnamji did not regain consciousness until the next day. "What time is it? Where is Swamiji?" he asked.

"It is 1 in the afternoon. Swamiji left for India yesterday at about 9 in the morning. He was very upset to leave you here. We took you to the doctor; then I urged him to continue with his plan, so he departed in an indecisive mood. He left this blanket for you, and it is a good thing that he did because we did not have anything warm to cover you with. You have been unconscious for a long time. How do you feel?" I asked.

"Dead," he replied. "What a pity that I could not say good-bye to Swamiji. You should have tried to arouse me. I must apologize when I next see him."

Just as his even mindedness was unchanging, so was his humility. Because I became angry at the slightest provocation and still thought very highly of myself, I wondered if I would be able to emulate Ratnamji's example in this lifetime. I felt like a mosquito aspiring to cross the ocean. Ratnamji took the homeopathic medicine regularly for the next two days and felt well enough to travel on the date fixed for our journey. "It looks as if God is gracious towards us or else I would have been laid up for a long time. Now He is giving us a chance to see if my leg is healed," he said.

The same day, we took the plane to Pokhara and searched for a place to stay. There was a Kali temple perched on a hilltop on the outskirts of the village. It meant a tough climb, but the atmosphere there would be very peaceful. Kali is the fierce aspect of the Divine Mother. The Divine Mother Herself is the Power of God in an embodied form. She has three functions and three aspects pertaining to creation, preservation, and destruction. Whatever is created must ultimately be destroyed. Kali is that aspect of God's Power which destroys every created object. Sarasvati is the Creative Power and Laxmi is the Power of Preservation. Kali is worshipped by worldly people to destroy obstructions to their happiness like ill health, poverty, or enemies. Spiritual aspirants worship Kali for the destruction of their spiritual ignorance, which veils the Reality within and makes one feel limited to a body and mind. Although every Hindu knows that God, the Supreme Being, is One and formless, he also believes that God can and does manifest in infinite forms for the convenience and joy of His devotees. One person may be called mother, sister, daughter, and niece by different people depending upon the relationship with each. Yet the person is one and the same. Viewed by different minds, the One Being is called Divine Mother, Krishna, Siva, and a myriad of other names.

After cooking our food and worshipping Mother Kali, we finished our lunch and started to walk north inquiring on our way about the route to Muktinath. We had decided to do our own cooking, so we had carried a kerosene stove, kerosene, rice, and other foodstuffs, as well as our clothes and bedding. It was quite a formidable weight, and we decided to hire three porters to help us and to show the way. At that time, we did not know that we should hire only Nepali porters. We had one bitter experience after another due to our ignorance. The first place that we had found any hired labor was in the Tibetan refugee camp outside the village. We met with three men there, agreed upon wages, and decided to start the next morning.

At sunrise we started on the road to Muktinath. Road is hardly the word for the foot path leading into the Himalayas to Muktinath 85 miles away. Muktinath is only a short distance from the border of China. Beyond Pokhara there was no road. Ratnamji and Seshamma, his sister, decided to walk the whole distance barefoot as a religious austerity. I also wanted to walk barefoot, but had stepped on a sharp piece of wood the previous night and cut the bottom of my foot. Thus, I had to wear rubber thongs, which later proved to be a source of great suffering for me.

A few miles beyond Pokhara, the ascent into the Himalayan foothills started. The climb was steep and exhausting, but the breathtaking scenery and pure air more than compensated for the exertion. The porters were walking so fast that we did not see them after the first hour. This was a foretaste of what was to come. Ratnamji had warned me that we should not hire the men who had come to our room the previous night seeking work. For some reason he did not like their appearance. I had insisted that there was no other way, and we had at last hired them.

Fortunately, by noon, we found our guides waiting for us in a small village on the side of a mountain. They were already cooking their food. We asked them why they had gone so far ahead of us. We explained that we did not know the way and depended on them to show us the path. They said that we were walking too slowly and that they could not slow down for our sake. We told them that if they could not walk with us, they had better go back. They promised to walk slowly.

After cooking and eating, we set out for the next village, hoping to arrive before nightfall. Only forests lie between Himalayan villages, and if you do not reach a village before sunset you risk being attacked by wild animals. That night we somehow managed to reach the next village, but being too tired to cook, we simply purchased some milk and cookies, ate them, and went to sleep. During the next three weeks, we found it surprising that a glass of milk in the morning, a full meal at noon, and milk and a few cookies at night were sufficient to keep us going. In fact, our health was much better while climbing in the mountains and our minds remained in an elevated state without any effort, perhaps due to the exercise and air. Our midday meal was extremely simple. We threw rice, lentils, and unripe bananas into a pot and boiled the whole thing together, adding salt at the end. Neither before nor after this pilgrimage did I ever taste such delicious food. We clearly experienced that hunger is the real sauce.

For two or three days, everything went smoothly. Then the porters again started to speed up and leave us behind. On one occasion, they disappeared into the distance taking even our flashlight with them. There was nothing left with us but a little money. We shouted and shouted but to no avail. As we walked along, we came to a fork in the trail. We took the left fork, which led to a dead end. We wasted two hours in backtracking. It was already nearly 5 in the evening, and we did not know how far away the next village was. There was no one to show us the way.

I decided to hurry ahead and try to find the porters, so I quickened my pace. Ratnamji and Seshamma were resting by the side of the path. In my eagerness to find the porters and our belongings, I neglected to leave some money with Ratnamji. A little voice inside me told me to leave them some money, but I ignored it and went ahead. It has always been my experience that when I fail to listen to that voice within, something painful has to follow, and it certainly did this time. Before long I came to a stone wall obstructing the path. The only other way led into a thick forest. It was already getting dark. I thought that perhaps the village lay in the forest and proceeded. After I went about 1/4 mile, a man suddenly appeared coming from the other direction. "Where are you going? Don't you know that you are walking into a thick forest?" the man said in English.

In Nepal there were very few people who spoke English in those days, even in the cities, and here I was in the middle of a forest in the Himalayan foothills being accosted by a stranger speaking perfect English. My surprise was forgotten at my joy of finding someone who seemed to know the way. I told him I was lost, that my porters had abandoned me, and that I was searching for them. I also told him about Ratnamji and Seshamma whom I had left behind.

"Follow me," the stranger said. "I will find your porters and give them a good scolding."

Although it was pitch dark by that time, he briskly walked in the direction from which I had just come but took a turn off somewhere along the way. I had to stumble in order to keep up with him. After fifteen minutes of exhausting climbing and crossing a raging river, we came to a village. The gentleman asked me to sit in front of a house while he went up and down the streets shouting for the porters. He at last found them and gave them a good upbraiding. He then ordered them to take all of our belongings to a house where we could stay comfortably. Then it started to rain heavily. I was utterly exhausted, but what to do about Ratnamji and Seshamma? I realized that they did not have any money with them. I told the gentleman, and taking a raincoat, my flashlight, and one of the porters, he went in search of them. I lay down exhausted and fell asleep.

In the middle of the night I awoke to see Ratnamji and Seshamma coming into the room soaking wet. Without even changing their clothes or uttering a word, they lay down and fell asleep. I also fell back asleep. The next morning, Ratnamji did not move. I saw that he was awake, but he would not answer my inquiries. He lay there until 11 or 12 o'clock. Finally, I pleaded with him to say something, though apprehensive of what he would say.

"How could you abandon us like that without even leaving us a little money? I did not realize that you were so cruel. My estimation of you must have been completely wrong," he said in a voice mixed with pain and anger.

"I had no intention of abandoning you. I thought that I should try to find the village and the porters and then go back with the flashlight and find you. If all three of us were lost in the darkness what could we do? If at least one of us reached the village, he could go back and get the others with a light. That was my plan. Unfortunately, by the time I realized that I had left you without any money, I was already far ahead. I thought that I would not be able to reach the village if I turned back, so I kept going. Somehow a stranger found me in the forest and took me to the village. After finding the porters, he sent them looking for you. I would have come myself, but I was so exhausted I couldn't walk another step and fell asleep on the spot. Please forgive me. I didn't leave you with any bad intention," I explained.

Having come to know the truth, Ratnamji got up and cleaned his teeth and washed his face. After drinking a glass of milk, he became his usual self. He then narrated to me what had happened after I had left them.

"After you left, sister and I tried to follow you but you were going too fast. I saw you shout something back at us, but I could not make out what you were saying. We also hurried our pace and somehow reached the bank of a rushing river by the time darkness had set in. We had no idea where we were or what direction to take. Seshamma and I got into the river, but she slipped and was almost washed away in the current. With great difficulty I caught her. We reached the other side of the river more dead than alive. Exhausted and hungry, we came to a house at the outskirts of the village. I explained to the owner that we had no money and were hungry. Seeing our pitiful condition, he divided his supper with us, though poor himself. By that time, our porter and another gentleman arrived inquiring about us and slowly brought us here in the rain. I was sure that Seshamma would be washed away in that river, and that was my main worry. What would her husband say? Anyhow, you should have left some money with us. We have arrived only by God's grace. What shall we do with these rascals, our porters?"

I said that we should get rid of them. However, the lady who owned the house in which we were staying informed us that no porters were available in the village. She also cautioned us to be extremely careful as some pilgrims who had recently taken porters from the same place had mysteriously disappeared between the two villages. It was suspected that they were murdered and their money taken. She seemed genuinely concerned for our safety.

Ratnamji called the porters and told them we would not travel that day. He also threatened that if they played any more mischief they would be dismissed. They knew, of course, that we were bluffing as no other porters would be available. They were hard-hearted and calculating. That evening, they came to us and said that if we did not increase their wages, they would not carry our things. What could we do? We had to agree.

The following day, we resumed our journey. Due to the rain the path had become very dangerous, with occasional landslides on the way. At one point, as we were slowly making our way along the side of a mountain with a river raging 1,000 feet below, a group of men appeared coming from the other direction. Though it was a one-lane road, we had to make it into a double-lane highway or someone would have to go for a swim! The men were adamant that they should be allowed to pass on the mountain side and that we should pass on the river side. While we cautiously performed this maneuver, with bated breath, my foot slipped on the loose soil. I thought that everything was over. Somehow I managed to catch hold of some long grass growing nearby and was saved from tumbling to my death. We were told that the day before a horse had slipped at the same spot and had painted the rocks with its blood. Needless to say, the poor creature was never seen again but disappeared into the raging current below.

One night, having covered about half the distance to Muktinath, we took rest in a village. During the night, I awoke to hear Ratnamji loudly chanting some verses; then he fell back to sleep. In the morning, he told me that he had a vision in the night of a temple with a huge discover wheel carved in stone in front of it. There were priests coming from the river with pots of water on their heads and he heard loud chanting of the Divine Name Marayana. Suddenly, he found himself sitting up in the room, but the sound Marayana, was still reverberating in his ears. It was at that time that I had heard him chanting the verses in praise of God as Marayana. He told me that when he had gone on pilgrimages before, he had similar experiences when he was within a certain distance of an intended temple. He then knew that he was in the jurisdiction, so to speak, of the deity of that temple.

As we walked further and further, the vegetation became more and more sparse. Finally, we were in an absolutely desolate region. There was not a single tree and only some small, almost leafless, bushes here and there. The Napal government had given me a permit to walk only up to Jomsom, about eight or 10 miles south of Muktinath. There was an Indian army base there keeping watch on the Chinese, and they did not want any foreigners going beyond that point. I pleaded with the officials and they were very sympathetic, but they could not permit me to go further. Ratnamji told me not to worry, that he would come back within a few days and bring me the consecrated offerings, or prasad, from the temple. I stood at the outskirts of the town and watched him disappear into the distance.

After returning to the room in which I was lodging, I found that he had forgotten his blanket. How would it be possible for him to manage without a blanket in that cold, windy place? I went to the army camp, and met the officer in charge, and told him about it. He agreed to send me with one of his soldiers to catch up with Ratnamji, and we started off at a run. Nearly one hour and three miles later we reached him. The joy of seeing his face was worth the effort. This time not so disconsolate, I returned to Jomsom and awaited his arrival with an eager heart.

For the next four days, I kept myself as busy as if I were in the ashram at Arunachala. Getting up in the early morning, I would bathe in an ice cold spring near the army barracks and then do my daily worship or puja. Cooking and eating took up some time, and I spent the rest of the day studying and meditating. At last, Ratnamji returned.

"If you think that our journey to this place was difficult, you should have been with us up to Muktinath," he said. "I was sure that I would never see you again. After leaving you the second time, we came to a pass where the wind was so fierce we thought we would be blown into the gorge below. First we tried walking through, but that was impossible. Then we tried crawling on all fours, but even that was not possible. Finally, we decided to wait until the next day, and we camped that night in the open. The cold was terrible. The next day the wind subsided, and we hurried through the pass. Just as we got through, the wind started to blow again with a howling sound.

Somehow we reached Muktinath. To my surprise, I found it to be the same temple I had seen in my vision. Even the huge wheel carved in stone was there at the entrance. We worshipped there and arranged a feast for the two priests who were staying there. When asked what their favorite dish was, they replied milk pudding, so we asked them to arrange to get some milk from the next village. They brought about four gallons of milk the next day in which we boiled rice and sugar to make pudding for the priests. They wanted nothing else. You can imagine the quantity of pudding that four gallons of milk made! They were voracious eaters, and we were happy to satisfy their desire. We felt we were feeding God Himself in their form. After that I went down to the river and collected those saligram stones. I could not make out which were good ones and which were not, so I simply brought about 200 of them. Here are the remains of the puja offerings."

We decided to start back for Pokhara the next day after Ratnamji and his sister had rested. We started early the next morning after taking leave of the army personnel. A small boil had formed on the top of my foot where my rubber thongs had rubbed. Now the boil was increasing in size. By the time we had walked three days, the boil had increased so much I could not walk. My foot was swollen to the size of a football.

"Well, what are we to do now?" I asked. "You go ahead and leave me here. When I am better I will somehow meet you at Pokhara."

"A very nice solution indeed! Am I so selfish as to leave you here alone?" Ratnamji retorted. "Some other way must be found. We shall ask one of the porters to carry you on his back at least down to the next village."

With great difficulty and much grumbling from the porters, we reached the next village about four miles away. The pain was unbearable. That night Seshamma applied a hot poultice to the boil, but I did not feel any relief. Ratnamji inquired in the village if there was anyone who could carry me back to Pokhara, a distance of about thirty-five miles. There was no one. We had no choice but to push on as we were doing.

In the morning, Ratnamji suggested that he and Seshamma start early, go slowly to the next village, and start the cooking. I should come along later with the porters, one of them carrying me. I agreed and so they left. I waited until 10 o'clock and then limped out in search of the porters.

They were sitting under a tree in front of the house.

"Why haven't we started yet?" I asked.

"We do not want to carry you, and we do not want to carry your luggage either. If you raise our wages, we will somehow carry the luggage, but under no circumstances are we going to carry you. You can do as you like," they replied.

Oh Ramana, why are you playing like this with me? Is this how you treat your devotees? All right. I will give them the money and walk and somehow reach Ratnamji on my own. Thinking thus, I gave them the money they asked for and we started. They, of course, left me behind within a few minutes. I was left to myself with an eight-mile walk ahead of me, down a mountain side through a forest in the hot sun, with a throbbing foot.

As I walked, I tried to be as happy as I had seen Ratnamji in similar painful situations. Here was a real chance to practice surrender to God. If I would stop walking even for a minute the pain in the foot would become so unbearable that I would scream out. At one point after limping along for about four miles, I stopped exhausted. The foot started to throb, and I thought it would burst. I screamed "Amma" at the top of my voice, calling to the Divine Mother. Immediately, the pain stopped. "What is this wonder?" I thought. As I continued on to the next village, I did not feel the pain as much. I thanked God for His mercy.

As soon as Ratnamji saw me, he jumped up and asked, "What is the matter? What have those rascals done to you?" I told him the whole story. Neither before nor after that have I ever seen Ratnamji so angry. He cursed those porters that they should find an abode in the lowest hell after their deaths, and I had no doubt that they would. Great saints have the power to curse as well as bless. It is very rare that they would curse anyone, and certainly would not do it for their own benefit. Ratnamji felt so pained at my suffering that he could not control his anger. I could only think, may God have pity on those poor fellows who are the objects of that anger.

Fortunately, there was a man in that village willing to carry me to Pokhara. He purchased a large basket, cut out one side of it so that I could sit in it, and put a blanket inside. He carried me on his back with a strap of cloth supporting the basket and slung over his forehead. In that way both his hands were free. I felt very awkward, to say the least, and pressed Ratnamji and Seshamma to hire porters also, but they would hear nothing of it. This mode of travel was very slow, especially since the man had to carry me up and down two mountains in the rain. I felt extremely sorry for him. He never complained and kept inquiring if I needed anything. What a vast difference from the other porters! Ratnamji and his sister made their way quickly. The porter and I followed slowly and met them for lunch. We met again each night.

It took us only two days to reach Pokhara. On the way, the boil burst giving me some relief though I had no medicine to dress the wound. After reaching Pokhara, we paid off the porters, giving the porter who had carried me an additional bonus. Luckily, three seats were available on the next plane to Kathmandu and we reached the capitol city that same evening.

After attending to my wound, we purchased tickets to India. Our bitter experience with the porters had created a keen interest in returning to India, and we eagerly looked forward to tomorrow.

Chapter 4

PILGRIMAGE

India! For all its heat, feverish activity, and poverty, still it is my home, and I was glad to be back. Although I liked Nepal, on the few occasions when I thought I would never see India again, I could not bear the thought. Nepal is a holy land, no doubt, but for me India is even holier.

Most of the tourists who come to India are appalled at the poverty, sickness, and general unkempt appearance of the people and the country. Nowadays, with many Indians going abroad for work, even some of the Indian people look down on their own country, considering America and other western nations as heaven on earth. Anything foreign is good; anything Indian is useless. This is the present day feeling of most of the Indian people.

Having lived half my life in America and half in India, I know both sides of the coin. The Indian people, blinded by the glitter of materialism, fail to see the venomous side of the west and the unique grandeur of their own culture. Rape, murder, theft, and general hooliganism are rampant in America. If one were to compare the per capita crime rates in the two countries, I think one would find that India's crime rate is a drop in the ocean of America's. This is certainly not due to the difference in law enforcement techniques, which are far superior in the West.

The idea of leading a virtuous life and the fear of reaping the consequences of evil deeds in this or another life are deep rooted in the Indian mind. There is not one Indian who does not know at least a little about the ancient Hindu Scriptures such as the classic *Ramayana* and *Mahabharata*. These works were written by sages who had attained the height of God-Realization and wanted to share their Bliss and knowledge with all mankind. They found that their knowledge and experience could best be spread through stories. The characters depicted in those works manifest the highest and noblest human qualities. The ancient sages encouraged the people to emulate sublime qualities in their own lives and, using a scientific system, showed that the true purpose of life is not pleasure but the Bliss and Peace borne out of Realization of one's True Nature. They also instilled the idea that peaceful coexistence should be the ideal on earth. These ideas and the subsequent way of life have been followed for thousands of years and, in spite of the onslaught of foreign invaders, the ancient culture stood in its purity until recent times.

The influence of mass communication has all but spoiled the ancient culture of India. The western ideals of enjoyment and pleasure has gripped the simple, childlike minds of the Indian people. Consequently, they have forgotten the greatness of their own culture. It is curious to note, however, that the people of the west are becoming disillusioned with their own self-destructive, materialistic culture in increasing numbers and are turning towards India, the mother of Hinduism and Buddhism, to satisfy their spiritual hunger. Being one such person, I overlooked the poverty of India as a superficial coat of paint and saw instead the wonderful spiritual culture lying beneath it. I have found that if one wants to attain God Vision and peace of mind, India is the best place on earth to do this because of its heritage and spiritual legacy. Though I hear people praising America day and night for its material advancement, I take no heed of their words, any more than I would to children's prattle. Even the study of quantum physics, after the investment of huge amounts of money and time, has produced the same conclusions that Indian sages arrived at thousands of years ago through the power of meditation.

For example, they knew that the universe is a unified whole comprised of essential energy and that the consciousness of the observer affects the observed phenomenon. This is one of the basic teachings of the Vedanta philosophy. The fact that the universe consists of energy and consciousness was pithily expressed by the sages in a pictorial way as Shiva Shakti, the Supreme Being in the duel form of Static Awareness and Dynamic Energy. Any Hindu child can tell you that this world is Shiva Shakti

Maya, or consists of Shiva and Shakti! It is gratifying to see that the ancient Indian culture is slowly being recognized and is being resuscitated at least by foreigners. As one great Indian sage recently said, "Hindus will follow Hinduism only if the foreigners do!"

After arriving in India we journeyed to Durgapur, one of the main steel producing centers in India, where Seshamma's husband and son were staying. Ratnamji wanted to accompany them on a further pilgrimage to the nearby places of Goya, Benaras, and Allahabad. After a few days in Durgapur, we took a train to Goya and reached there the next day.

From the time that I left Tiruvannamalai to come to Hyderabad, I had enjoyed much peace of mind and had a harmonious relationship with Ratnamji. After going through the fire during the first year with him, I became very alert so as not to make any mistakes. If he told me to do a thing, I would try to do it unquestioningly. The split tendency of my mind had greatly subsided, and as a result, I was able to grasp the meaning and value of what he was advising. I tried to forget myself in serving him. I felt that everything should be done perfectly if I were to please him and get the grace of God. In fact, I forgot about everything else, and at that time only he, Ramana, and I existed, so to speak, in my mind.

It was really wonderful how my meditation became spontaneous when I followed his instructions. I felt an inner Oneness with him in my heart. I started to listen to my heart instead of my mind and tried to make the resultant peace a permanent and continuous experience. It had been increasing as the days went by, and I noticed that it was usually only due to my foolishness that I would lose it. I was confident that by alert application to the principles he taught me I would reach my goal.

Goya is the most important place in India for the worship of one's ancestors. It is believed that one has a duty to one's departed ancestors and that one should appease them once a year by feeding a scriptural scholar as their representative. The ceremony is done with the accompaniment of mantras or mystic formulas which, much like telegrams, ensure that the subtle portion of the food will somehow reach the ancestors, wherever they are. With present-day radio, TV, and satellite communications, it is not difficult to conceive how subtle objects can be transported to another being by mantric power, which is only another form of energy.

I also took part in the worship and felt satisfied that at least once in my life I had discharged this duty. I was sure that nothing the ancients had recommended could be unnecessary. They were established in a state which transcends time and space, and as such, their realizations are applicable for all times and places.

The goal of life and the problems of life never seem to change in essence, though differences in time and place may appear, to an undiscerning mind, to alter the goal and the problems. Ramana clearly told that happiness is the goal of man, and everyone experiences this to be so. However, by seeking happiness through worldly means, one can never find it, and it actually recedes further. Only when the mind has been calmed can peace be attained; perfect peace and eternal happiness are one and the same. Regardless of our circumstances, we must be rooted in an internal peace so that nothing is able to disturb our inner balance. Though extremely simple to understand, the practices leading to such a state are most difficult, because of the complex and restless nature of the mind. Conceivably, one may succeed through trial and error to find the way to calm the mind. A much shorter path is to follow the teachings of the saints and sages whose minds are established in the stillness of Reality.

After staying in Goya for a day, we continued on to Donaras, or Kasi as it is more commonly called. This is considered to be the stronghold of Hindu culture, and rightly so. Every year, millions of people make a pilgrimage to this holy place to worship God in the temple and to take a purifying bath in the holy Ganges River. Donaras could very well be called the Jerusalem of India. It was in Kasi that I experienced clearly that God exists, not as a matter of faith, but as a direct experience in the core of my being.

Ratnamji, Seshamma, and her husband had a strong desire to do the traditional rituals pertaining to a pilgrimage to Kasi. It was decided that I would have more freedom if given separate accommodations. I stayed in a room in the house of the priest who was going to assist in the rituals, while they were accommodated in a guest house near the river. Though I did not like to be separated from Ratnamji, he promised to meet me every night. In fact, this arrangement proved to be a blessing in disguise.

Every morning I would got up at 3:30 and went to the river. At that hour, there were very few people at the bathing ghats. The Ganges seemed to be alive. I greeted Her and asked permission to bathe in Her water. I had great faith in the purifying power of the Ganges and looked upon Her as a Goddess. Even medical science has found the antiseptic power of Ganges water to be so potent that cholera and other deadly germs are unable to survive in it. Saints over the ages, spiritual scientists, had testified to the spiritually purifying effect of the river and had called Her holy. They no doubt had some experience which made them believe so. This is most probable, for I was shortly to have such an experience myself.

After bathing each morning, I came back to my room and meditated for a short time. Then I walked to the Siva Temple about a mile away through narrow, winding lanes. Even at that early hour, many people were awake and going to the temple. After catching a glimpse of the deity, I slowly made my way back to my room, purchasing flowers for my worship on the way. I preferred to get lotus flowers, and these were available in the market only in the early morning. After reaching my room, I performed the worship and then read the stories of Lord Siva from the Scriptures. The form of God which presided over the city of Kasi, or Donaras, was Siva, or Lord Vishveshwara, meaning the Lord of the Universe. Ratnamji usually came to my room later and, after we talked for some time, he took me to the different temples and holy places in and around Kasi. I spent each afternoon studying, and each night Ratnamji returned and took me to one of the bathing ghats, where we would have spiritual discussions until late at night.

In the third week of our stay, I had a dramatic experience. One morning, after returning from the temple, I sat down for my usual daily worship. I was nearly finished and was singing the Divine Name of Siva when suddenly the awareness of my body and surroundings totally vanished; what remained was, for lack of a better word, God. I was overwhelmed by the sense of the reality of God's Presence. In some inexplicable way, I was one with It and, at the time, a little separate from It.

After some time, I slowly became vaguely aware of my body and clearly felt the Divine Presence as if It was blissfully dancing on the top of my head. Afraid to lose that Bliss, I kept my eyes shut. I could hear myself shouting "Siva Siva" in a loud voice, but it seemed quite separate from me. Gradually, the intensity of that Bliss decreased, and the awareness of my body and surroundings became more clear. I slowly opened my eyes to find that my clothes and face were drenched with tears, although I had not had the least awareness of having wept. I sat there stunned and overjoyed at this sudden manifestation of Divine Grace. Just then, Ratnamji walked in. One look at my face made him understand what had happened.

"I think I have seen God," I said.

"Such is the effect of bathing every day in the Ganges with faith in its spiritual power," he replied smiling. "If one is sincere about spiritual life and bathes regularly in the Ganges, some experiences should come. In any case, mental purity and innocence will be greatly enhanced. Now you have experienced the truth of the sages words."

I had already been convinced of the truth of the ancients' words. Now there was not the least doubt about it. What had happened to me was as clear as daylight. Even as I write these words, 15 years later, I can still remember that day's event as if it was only yesterday.

Our stay in Kasi had come to a close and a very auspicious one at that, at least for me. The next day we were to proceed to Allahabad, or Prayag as it is traditionally called, the place where the Ganges and Yamuna rivers meet. It is said that to bathe in that place is very helpful for spiritual aspirants, and I was looking forward to reaching there. I was, of course, happy to once again be with Ratnamji all of the time.

The next day we took a train to Allahabad and got off on the Ganges side of the railway bridge at a small village named Jbusi where the ashram of Swamiji's Guru, Prabhudattaji, is located. Ratnamji thought that would be the best place for us to stay. While we were going along the road in a horse-drawn cart, Ratnamji asked me to get out at the post office and inquire as to the exact whereabouts of the ashram. As I entered the post office, who should I see but Swamiji! I went to bow down to him but he caught me up in an embrace.

"Where is Ratnamji?" he asked. I took him to the cart and we all joyfully made our way to the ashram of his Guru. He had us comfortably accommodated and then brought Prabhudattaji, a very stoutly built man with long white hair and a beard haphazardly sticking out in all directions. He had the eyes of a crazy man. He was indeed crazy with the Bliss of God-Consciousness! We all bowed down to him. Then he took us to the kitchen and sat with us while we had our lunch. He gave me a name, Neolamani, which is an epithet of Krishna's meaning blue gem. He had written about 150 books on spiritual subjects, all very informative and entertaining, putting the Truth in a very sweet and lively form. In the evening, he read portions from some of the books and explained them. His conversations were very animated.

Prabhudattaji told us a funny story about a rich man whose daughter had come to his ashram. Her father insisted that she should return to the house and not visit the ashram. He told her, "I have three cars and your Guru also has three cars. I am the owner of so many buildings and so is your Guru. He seems to have much wealth just like me. Then what is the difference between us? Why go there? You might as well stay here." The girl went to Prabhudattaji and told him what her father had said. He summoned her father and gave him a comfortable seat.

"You rascal!" he said. "Did you say that we are equals? Do you want to know what is the difference between us? I can get up at any minute and walk away from all this without even a set of clothes and never even give it a thought afterwards as long as I live. What is the case with you? Even to spend an insignificant amount of money makes you feel a great loss! That is the difference between us. That is why your daughter wants to stay with me and not with you!" It seems that the light dawned on this man, and he presented the ashram with a huge sum of money to arrange a religious festival for thousands of poor people.

Every day, we took a boat and went to bathe at the place where the Yamuna and Ganges meet. Prabhudattaji told us that every 12 years a festival was held here which was attended by nearly 15 million people each day. I could hardly believe my ears. Fifteen million people? He invited us to come for the next festival which would take place in about six years. I did, in fact, attend that festival, which was called the Kumbha Mela. There was no exaggeration about the number of people there. The crowd was inconceivably large, stretching for miles in both directions on the dried-up riverbed. It was virtually a city, without the crime of a city. There was not even one case of theft, fighting, or any kind of violence. The entire crowd was all of one mind, gathered for the express purpose of bathing in the river.

My visa was about to expire. I had to leave for Tiruvannamalai before our pilgrimage was completed. Ratnamji and Swamiji told me to meet them back in Hyderabad after renewing my visa. After taking leave of them, I departed for the south. After completing my visa formalities, I again journeyed to Hyderabad and met Ratnamji and Swamiji. For the next two years, I traveled to different parts of India in the company of these two holy men. To be with them was a continuous festival and learning process. Their patience with me, who knew nothing of spirituality and who committed blunder after blunder through body, speech, and mind, was unlimited. Though I looked upon them as my spiritual guides, they looked upon me only as their younger spiritual brother.

For many years, past devotees had wanted to construct a house for Ratnamji, but he had repeatedly refused. Now his health was starting to fail him, and he felt that a permanent residence might become necessary. He agreed to the persistent demand of his friends and admirers. With some money from his brother, he purchased a small plot of land near the ashram in Tiruvannamalai. At that time, he asked if I planned to stay there permanently. I wanted to be with him as long as he was alive and answered in the affirmative.

Strangely, the plot adjoining his came up for sale. The owner had to perform his daughter's marriage and was in need of money. He asked me if I wanted to purchase the plot, and I immediately agreed. Plans were drawn up for two small houses, and with the money given by devotees and money I had recently inherited, the construction began. During the next year, although Ratnamji continued his travels, I remained in Tiruvannamalai supervising the construction work. It should have taken only a few months, but frequent inclement weather, labor problems, and a shortage of materials caused the work to drag on for nearly a year. At last it was finished, and Ratnamji promised to return soon.

Although both houses were completed simultaneously, Ratnamji advised me through letters that it was not a good time to do the house-opening ceremony of his house, but that mine could be done at once. He wrote that I should request my mother to come to India for the function, that in the person of one's mother abides a special manifestation of Divine Power, the power of affection which helps preserve and nourish the creation. He mentioned that as soon as I had set the date, he would try to come, along with Swamiji. I immediately wrote to my mother requesting her to come for the ceremony and mentioned that only on hearing from her about her arrival date could I fix the date of the function. It had been four years since she had seen me, and upon hearing from me, made arrangements immediately. She arrived within a few weeks, along with my stepfather. Ratnamji and Swamiji also arrived and stayed in the ashram. I accommodated my mother in the house of a devotee.

On the day before the function, I took my mother and stepfather to the ashram to meet Ratnamji and Swamiji. Some devotees of Swamiji from Madras were just leaving to return to their home. In India, one bows down to elders and holy men as a mark of respect and humility when meeting, as well as when leaving them. This is not done to flatter them. The ancients learned that every position or posture of the body affects the nervous system, which in turn affects the mind, or mental attitudes. Pointing one's index finger at someone while talking, for example, subtly increases one's feelings of self importance, arrogance, and perhaps anger as well. Likewise, bowing down to another person puts the mind in a receptive mood to receive advice from those who may be wiser than ourselves.

When my stepfather saw the gentlemen bowing down to Swamiji, he asked, "Why should one man bow down to another? Are we not all equals?" This, of course, is a universally accepted notion, but it is a fallacious one. Although the spark of Life or God is the same in everyone, everything else is different. Physically, mentally, morally, and spiritually, every man differs from the other. The universally equal thing in everyone is, unfortunately, uniformly overlooked and ignored, and only our differences are seen and stressed. I say unfortunate, because if our vision were one of Unity, this world would be a much more peaceful place. Ratnamji was not one to be caught unaware by anyone. He immediately asked a counter-question.

"When you want a promotion are you not bowing down to your boss, though perhaps in another way? These men want the knowledge and experience they feel we have. In order to get that, they are bowing down. That, of course, is not enough, but it is a first step. Whether the mind is bowing down must still be seen. A nonreceptive mind cannot be taught anything." My stepfather, perhaps realizing the truth of these words, kept quiet. After a few minutes of conversation, they left for their room.

Ratnamji and I then discussed the house-opening plans. In India one does not "warm" a house but rather enters as a beginning. This is a religious function, and it is believed that if certain rites are done in the house before living in it, the initial vibrations will make the atmosphere conducive to a peaceful and harmonious life in the house. It is also told that the shape of the house and the direction it faces also affect the occupants in positive or negative ways. This was considered true by all ancient cultures. Perhaps scientific research will find some day that it is so, though these principles are based on extremely subtle laws of vibrations, or wave of energy which pervades the universe affecting events and mental changes.

We decided that Swamiji would enter the house first to the accompaniment of the chanting of Vedic mantras, and then certain rituals would be performed. Finally, all the guests would be fed, thus ensuring the good will of every-one present. Ratnamji thought that asking Swamiji to enter the house first would make the house more helpful for spirit-ual practice. As it turned out, God had His own plan, which was quite different from ours but no doubt was for the best.

The next morning, we all assembled at the ashram. Then we slowly walked to the new house singing the Di-vine Name. On the way, a stranger took my mother aside and told her that, as she was my mother, she must enter the house first. Those words were not heard by any of us. As we approached the front door, the priests started chanting the Vedic mantras. Swamiji was just about to step into the house when, zoom, my mother rushed from the sidelines, pushed Swamiji aside, and triumphantly stepped into the house first! We all looked at each other in shock and sur-prise. Then Ratnamji laughed and said, "Apparently God wanted to enter first in the form of the mother!" This was happily accepted by all present, and everything else went smoothly.

My mother and stepfather wanted me to tour north India with them, so we left the next day. As we were leaving, Ratnamji told me that he was going to Bombay with Swamiji and that I should meet them there after my mother had gone. He gave me the address of the house where they would be staying. Promising to meet him, I left for Madras.

We visited most of the important tourist places in north India, and then my mother and stepfather returned to Ameri-ca, leaving me in Bombay. I immediately proceeded to the house where Swamiji and Ratnamji were staying. Bowing to them, I narrated all of the details of my journey. They then told me that they were invited to Baroda, a large city to the east of Bombay, by some devotees and would be leav-ing the next day. I had just come in time to accompany them.

The next day found us in Baroda by evening. Swami-ji went in search of a tablist or drummer to play during his evening singing. He went to the Music Academy, be-cause he did not personally know someone in Baroda who could play the drums. While he was inquiring there, he came across his music teacher of 40 years earlier. He had not seen the teacher since, and they had a happy reunion.

The teacher took us to his house. He was teaching sitar in the music school, where he showed us a painting of his teacher and told us that the painting was so rare he had to pay a huge amount of money to get it out of a private collection. As his teacher was his Guru, he spared no effort and worked hard for a long time to get enough money to pay for the painting. He played the sitar for us for about an hour, during which time Swamiji and Ratnamji both became deeply absorbed in meditation.

On a previous occasion, someone had invited Ratnamji to hear a concert by Ravi Shankar in Hyderabad. They asked me to come along. On the way, Ratnamji told me, "Don't get lost in the tune you hear. Keep your attention on the underlying drone note. Then the concert will be useful for meditation." We sat down in the auditorium and the lights went out. The concert began and I closed my eyes trying to concentrate on the drone. After what seemed like two minutes, the lights went on and everyone got up. I wondered what was the matter. Why had the concert been stopped at the very beginning? I looked at Ratnamji questioningly. Laughing, he said, "Come on, let's go. As soon as you closed your eyes, you fell fast asleep. That was two hours ago. I thought you must be very tired, so I did not disturb you. Such a deep meditation." Now, while listening to the sitar I make sure not to close my eyes.

After a few days stay in Baroda, Swamiji decided to go back to Bombay. Ratnamji had received a letter asking him to come to Hyderabad, so we purchased tickets to that place. At the time we purchased the tickets, I had to borrow the money from Swamiji as I had left my money at the house. When we reached Bombay, Swamiji got up to detrain. Ratnamji asked me, "How much do you owe Swamiji?" "Seventy dollars," I replied. "How much money do you have with you?" he asked. "A hundred and five," I replied.

"Give him a hundred," Ratnamji said. "It is a round figure. Besides it does not look nice to be so calculating while repaying a debt to a holy man." I grudgingly offered the money to Swamiji, who took it saying that he did not have any money with him and that the money would be useful. Then he got off the train at Bombay.

"Now what do I do?" I said, a bit irritated. "We still

have a journey of two days ahead of us. With five dollars, how will we purchase enough food for us?"

"Well, let us see how God provides for us. Should we not give Him an opportunity to do so now and then?" Ratnamji asked with a slightly mischievous grin on his face. "On the way, there are two holy places that I have been wanting to visit for a long time. One is Dehu Road where the Great Saint Tukaram lived about 300 years ago. Nearby is Alandi where the tomb of Jneshwar is located. He was a Realized Soul who voluntarily left his body at the age of 21 by asking his disciples to enter his body while he was still alive. He sat in meditation, suspending all of his vital functions, and was buried. Many devotees, even today, have seen him during meditation near his tomb, and some have been blessed with illuminating experiences.

The unfortunate thing is that this is an express train, and it will not stop at Dehu Road. On the other hand, if we get off at the next main stop, we can take a bus to Dehu Road and then come back to catch the next train. However, if we do that, we will not have a penny left to buy a banana. Well, let us see. Let us not eat today in order to save money."

Not eat? From the moment I heard those words, I started to think about how hungry I was. After a few hours, Ratnamji struck up a conversation with a man sitting on the same bench as us. The man had some grapes in a paper bag. Like a hungry wolf eyeing a flock of sheep, I kept my eyes glued to the bag. Oh great God in heaven! He was putting his hand in the bag and offering Ratnamji the grapes. Ah Lord, I knew that you would not let down your devotees! Ratnamji turned to me and opened his hands. Six small grapes. The man's generosity and my hunger were somehow out of proportion. Seeing my expression, Ratnamji burst into laughter. Personally, I could not see anything funny about it. God had let us down.

A few more hours and suddenly the train stopped. Ratnamji looked out the window. "Come on! Jump out! This is Dehu Road! God has stopped the train for us!" Ratnamji shouted. I hurriedly gathered the bags together and jumped out of the train. Immediately the train started. It seems that a cow had wandered on to the tracks, and the train was forced to stop until it moved out of the way. It just so happened to be Dehu Road!

We left our bag in a shop near the bus stand and went to see all of the places associated with the life of Tukaram. He had been a holy man who, though persecuted his whole life by ignorant people, always came out triumphant due to his innocent and pure heart. He instructed people in the spiritual life through songs he composed. His influence on the lives of people in that part of the country is felt even today. It is told that he mysteriously disappeared at the end of his life never to be seen again. His house and the temple where he sat and sang are preserved, and it was to these places that we went.

At one end of the town, there was a very old tree which seemed to be a sort of landmark, but as we could not speak the local languages, we could not make out what it was. Instead of feeling inspired thinking of the life of this sage, I was feeling hungry and a bit angry towards Ratnamji for having given away all of our money. We came back to the stop to catch the next bus to Alandi, about 20 miles away. The shopkeeper, who spoke English, told us that the bus would come in an hour. He asked us if we had seen the place from which Tukaram disappeared. He said that Tukaram had stood under a tree, and bidding farewell to all of his friends and well-wishers, disappeared in a blaze of light. Every year on the same day and at the same time the tree is supposed to violently quiver as if frightened. He told us where to find the tree.

Ratnamji said that we must see the tree before leaving, and he started out at a run in the burning noonday sun. It turned out that the tree that we had noticed earlier was the tree from which Tukaram had disappeared. By the time we got back to the shop, exhausted and thirsty, the bus had gone. I was grumbling under my breath. Our connecting train was at 6:00 p.m. and it was 1 o'clock. If we should miss the train our tickets would become invalid and we would be stranded without tickets or money.

The next bus to Alandi would come at 3 o'clock. After we went to Alandi, saw everything there and caught a bus to the train station, it would be almost 7:00 p.m. Besides, I was hungry and tired. Ratnamji, hearing that the bus would not come for two hours, lay down in the back of the shop, told me to wake him before 3, and fell asleep. This meant that I should not fall asleep. My mind was racing, due to anger and worry. Where was my surrender and trust in Ratnamji and Ramana? It had evaporated in the face of adversity.

Catching the bus at 3 o'clock, we arrived at Alandi at 4. We visited all the places associated with Jneshwar's life and finally sat for meditation near his tomb. Meditation? It was out of the question for me to meditate in such an agitated condition. We finally got on a bus which would take us to the train station in about two hours. Now God is going to teach a lesson to Ratnamji, I thought. Why should he be so impractical?

"How did you like those places? I felt as if transported to another world altogether, as if I was living with those saints. What about you?" Ratnamji asked.

"I am hungry and tired. How could I relish anything? Now it is also impossible for us to catch the train. If we had not gone to see that tree the second time, we would have been at the train station by now," I said in a tone of suppressed anger.

"It is a pity that you are thinking so much about your body, even after having lived with me for so long. Instead of using the pilgrimage for your spiritual betterment, you are using it only to spoil your mind. Where is your faith in Ramana if you cannot do without money for even one day? When we first met, you told me you wanted to live without money. Where is that spirit now?" he asked.

What could I say? He was right, as usual. At last the bus reached the train station, and we got out. In the station we were informed that our train was late and had not yet arrived! We rushed to the platform and reached there just in time to find our train arriving. After we found our seats, Ratnamji looked at me and smiled.

"Now purchase some bananas. Tomorrow we will reach our destination," he said. I had learned a good lesson and vowed never again to doubt my spiritual guide. Over the years, Ratnamji habitually came late to train stations, but he never missed a train.

In Hyderabad we learned that the Shankaracharya of

Puri had recently arrived and had arranged for a huge religious function. For two or three years, there had been no rain in Hyderabad, and the people had requested the Acharya to help them. It had been proven many times that, if certain Vedic sacrifices are performed strictly in accordance with scriptural injunctions, a heavy downpour of rain will occur immediately after the sacrifice. I have personally witnessed this twice, once in Tiruvannamalai and once in Hyderabad. It would take a long stretch of the imagination to say that, after two or three years of drought, the torrential downpour which occurred immediately following the sacrifice was a coincidence.

About 800 years ago, a boy call Shankara was born in the southern part of India. Even from his infancy, he showed signs of having a profound intellect. At the age of eight, he left his home and traveled by foot all over India until he found a Realized Guru and, studying under him, attained perfection. He then wrote commentaries on many of the Hindu scriptures for the benefit of sincere seekers and, before his death at the age of 32, established four or five ashrams in different parts of India, placing disciples he had trained in charge of these institutions. As he was a renowned teacher of religion he was called by the title Acharya.

From his time down to the present a continuous tradition has been handed down and each succeeding head is designated as the Shankaracharya. These men have been carefully chosen by their predecessors for their learning, austerity, devotion, and selflessness. They are the recognized leaders of a large portion of the Hindu population. The present Shankaracharya of Puri was one such outstanding personality renowned for his high spiritual achievements and devotion to God. He was, therefore, felt to be the best person to conduct the function.

The function consisted of two parts. Under one canopy, a meeting of all of the greatest scriptural scholars of India was held. During the day, these scholars discussed many controversial religious topics, quoting verses from the scriptures to win their points. At night, the Acharya would speak on various subjects which, although being of practical value to the ordinary man, would also better acquaint him with his religion and culture. Under the other canopy were constructed 1,000 fire pits in which various substances would be offered to God, using fire as the medium of worship accompanied by the recitation of Vedic mantras. This canopy was so huge that its circumference was about one mile. The sound of the mantras and the sight of the blazing fires were a feast to the ears and eyes. The atmosphere was charged with devotion. The rites would take 10 days to complete.

I very much wanted to have a personal interview with the Acharya and asked Ratnamji if this would be possible. Ratnamji knew the Acharya quite well and was spending most of his time in his presence. As a matter of fact, within a few days, Ratnamji became the Acharaya's personal attendant. The Acharya told Ratnamji that I should attend all of the discourses and that when he had time he would call me. For 10 days and nights from 6:00 a.m. until midnight, I sat expecting that I would be called any minute. At the end of 10 days the function was over, the rain had fallen, and I still had not been called.

The Acharya was due to leave Hyderabad that night for another city about 500 miles away. He sent a message saying that, if I still wanted to meet him, I could follow him to the next city. He was obviously testing my sincerity. I replied through the messenger that I would follow him all over India if necessary until he would meet me. The next day, as soon as he had finished his most urgent works, he summoned me, and in a closed room along with Ratnamji told me many things. He told me that, from ancient times onward, countless sages had attained Self-Realization through the constant repetition of the Divine Name. If I wanted to attain Supreme Bliss and Eternal Peace, that was the path to follow.

I was very happy to hear this, because Ratnamji had already told me to do this, and I was trying to follow that advice. After encouraging me to continue my efforts at Realization, the Acharya gave me, as a mark of his favor, the flowers and fruits that had been offered to God in his worship, or Puja. Bowing down to him, I took leave with a full and satisfied heart. It had been worth the wait of 10 days.

Ratnamji now advised me to go back to Tiruvannamalai

and make the necessary preparations for the opening of his house. He promised to meet me there in two weeks. I proceeded to Arunachala, and he accompanied the Acharya to north India, where he caught a cold. The cold eventually developed into a serious disease, which was largely responsible for his death three years later. This was the beginning of a very painful part of my spiritual life.

"Last night I had a very inauspicious dream. I think that from now on my health is going to be very bad," Ratnamji said while laying in my house. He had come with Seshamma, his sister, the previous night. He had a fever and a painful cough. While he was traveling, an abscess had developed on his foot and after causing much pain, had finally burst. He more or less had to be carried everywhere.

"Let us finish the opening ceremony somehow, and then we can go and consult a good doctor," he said. I was ready to go for a doctor as soon as I saw him, but he would not permit it. He felt that the doctor might put restrictions on him that would hinder the ceremony. Many people already had been invited and would be coming within a few days. If the date were to be changed, it would mean a lot of trouble and inconvenience for everyone.

We made all the necessary plans and arrangements for the function, and on the fixed day the rituals were performed by Ratnamji and the priests. About 50 guests had come from all over India, but Swamiji could not come. He was in the hospital with a heart attack, and the doctors would not permit him to move, much to his dismay. He had sent someone to convey the news personally to Ratnamji, who had been expecting him. After the worship, Ratnamji lay down. He was very weak and was having pains in his chest, but the usual smile and glow could be seen on his face. The next morning, we received word that a very old disciple of Ramana's was dying in the ashram. Ratnamji and I hurried to the ashram and found the monk on his deathbed. Everyone was chanting the Divine Name in a loud voice, and within a few hours, he peacefully left his mortal frame. His body was buried behind the ashram the same day, and it was decided that Ratnamji should do the 40 day worship of the tomb which is prescribed after the death of a monk. This meant another delay of 40 days until he could consult a doctor. My heart was breaking, but what could I do? He would not hear any arguments.

After 40 days of suffering, Ratnamji proposed that we go and see Swamiji who had been discharged from the hospital and was staying with some devotees. He promised to go to a doctor while we were there. Leaving Arunachala, we reached Swamiji and found his health slightly improved. However, he was having spasms in one of the main arteries near his heart and suddenly stood up gasping for breath a number of times a day. It was really painful to see him in that condition. As soon as an attack stopped, he would laugh and make jokes about it to us. After a few days, Ratnamji agreed to be taken to a doctor at Swamiji's insistence. An X-ray was taken and it was found that most of his lungs had been affected by tuberculosis. His blood sugar also was very high. In the evening, when the hosts found out what the nature of Ratnamji's sickness was, they felt worried and did not want to keep him in their house. Swamiji was extremely pained at their attitude. They warned him not to go too close to Ratnamji.

"If your own child should develop tuberculosis, would you stay away from him for fear of catching the disease? If there is real love, how can such thoughts occur?" Swamiji angrily retorted.

Swamiji, in a very gentle and tactful way, informed Ratnamji about the situation and suggested that we go to Hyderabad and admit him to the hospital there. Ratnamji also felt that this idea was best, but where would we get the money? We had spent everything on the house-opening ceremony, and now we did not have enough for train tickets or medicine. Ratnamji forbade me to mention this to Swamiji or anyone else. But within a few minutes, Swamiji came over to me and handed me a large sum of money.

"Keep this for Ratnamji's treatment," he said. "My Guru, Prabhudattaji, sent it to me hearing that I was sick. I don't need so much. It may be useful for you." My eyes filled with tears. Oh God, You are indeed looking after us, although I have doubted it again and again.

Swamiji said goodby, as we got into a taxi to go to the train station. We later learned that he had wept for nearly an hour because of the way Ratnamji had to be sent away and because of his own helplessness in not being able to come with us. In Hyderabad once again, we went to the outpatient clinic, where the doctors had a look at Ratnamji's lungs. "The person who has these lungs should certainly not have such a bright face!" exclaimed the doctors. This time Ratnamji was admitted into the men's medical ward. He would never agree to a private room or special treatment. What is the difference between the ordinary poor man and a monk? Should not a monk do with the minimum? Thinking thus, he wouldn't allow extra money to be spent on himself.

The area around his bed became, of course, an ashram. Almost all of the doctors and nurses would come to him with their problems, and though ordered to rest and not to talk much to give the lungs a chance to recuperate, he was made to talk 10 times more than if he had stayed outside the hospital!

"Let the body go to its own fate. Talking about God, my mind stays merged in Him and does not even think of the disease. What could be better than this? Who knows at what moment death will come? Should we not be thinking of Him at that time?" He would not heed our entreaties to talk less and take rest.

The inhuman cruelty of the doctors in the medical ward was not any less than we had experienced earlier in the surgical ward. One day a surgeon came into the ward with some of his students. Ratnamji was napping, and I was reading a book nearby. The doctor grabbed Ratnamji's foot and, with the handle of his reflex hammer, scraped the bottom of his tender feet, almost cutting through the flesh. Ratnamji screamed out. The doctor pointed out to his students, "You see, this is called reflex action." I was on the point of showing some of my reflex action to the merciless fellow when Ratnamji looked at me as if to say, "Don't touch him. He's ignorant."

On another day, a student was entrusted with the job of giving Ratnamji an injection. After sticking in the needle with a sudden jab, he said, "Oh my! It has gone in crooked." Without removing it, he simply bent it into position and, in the process, tore a half inch hole in Ratnamji's bottom. I could not restrain myself. I shouted at the man and chased him away from the bed. Ratnamji turned towards me and said, "Under no circumstances should you allow me to die in this hospital. It would be better to die in the hands of a butcher than here." If he had allowed us to keep him in a paying room, he would not have been treated like this, but as he was one of the "poor ones," it was permissible to treat him like a guinea pig.

During our two-month stay in the hospital, I was, as before, allowed to sleep by Ratnamji's bed. One night I had an unusual dream, or perhaps one could call it a vision. I saw an attractive room at the top of a flight of stairs and made my way up there. At that moment, a man accosted me and said, "There is a young girl here who is desirous of having a child. Would you mind obliging her?" Without thinking, I agreed to the man's proposal, but the next moment I realized what I had agreed to. Repenting for my foolishness and afraid that I might break my vow of celibacy, I ran down the stairs into the street. As I was running down the street, I noticed a temple beside the road and stopped in front of it. I could see the image of the Divine Mother inside. I started to cry out to Her, "Oh, Mother, forgive me for my stupidity!" As I was crying, the image of the Divine Mother suddenly disappeared, and standing in its place was the living Divine Mother in flesh and blood. She walked out of the temple, took me by the hand, and led me back to the room from which I had just escaped. Showing me some vulgar pictures hung on the wall, She said, "My child, this girl is not pure as you had thought. She is a very loose girl." Then She again took my hand and led me back to the temple. Leaving me at the entrance, She slowly moved backwards all the while looking lovingly at me and suddenly disappeared. In Her place was the stone image as before. Coming from the temple were strains of a song, "Victory to Mother, Victory to the Divine Mother."

Suddenly I awoke, but I was still hearing the song! After a few seconds, I realized that the song was coming from a radio in the corner of the ward. Just then, Ratnamji called, "Neal!" His voice was the same as that of the Divine Mother when she talked to me. I got up and told Ratnamji about the dream. He smiled and said, "You look upon me as the Divine Mother come to give you spiritual betterment. I also look upon you as the Divine Mother come to comfort my poor body. There are many ways to look at people. For example, you could consider me a sick person who needs help. Or you could consider me to be someone who is in a position to receive service from you. Another way would be to think of me as a devotee or a saint or even a sage and offer your services. But the highest and best way would be to consider that God is in the body of the person you serve and to offer your service feeling that you are fortunate to have an opportunity to serve Him. Ultimately your ego will become weakened, and God-Consciousness will dawn. Do not think that I am saying this for my own benefit. If you were not here, God would provide someone else to look after me. I depend solely on Him, not on any individual."

After two months in the hospital, Ratnamji's condition had improved greatly; no infection remained in his lungs. He was discharged and advised to continue the medicine for several days, being sure not to exert himself. Shortly after this, Swamiji sent word that a festival of continuous 24-hour singing of the Divine Name for one week would be conducted at a holy place called Bhadrachalam. He requested Ratnamji to come there as soon as possible.

Leaving Hyderabad we reached Bhadrachalam the next day and found Swamiji there in the company of hundreds of devotees. His health was much better, though he still had attacks now and then. During this festival, I hardly saw Ratnamji sleep, either in the day or in the night. He was always with the devotees singing, discussing spiritual topics, or following Swamiji here and there. The holy atmosphere of Bhadrachalam had a particularly intoxicating effect on both of them.

The existence of this temple was due solely to the efforts of a saint called Ramdas who lived about 200 years ago. He had a dream in which Sri Rama appeared before him and asked him to build a temple for His image which was sitting on the top of a hill without any protection. Ramdas was, at that time, a government officer in charge of collecting taxes and sending them to the emperor each year. Instead of remitting the taxes, he used the money for construction of the temple without informing the king.

This was discovered some years later. Ramdas was

made to walk three or four hundred miles in chains to a prison and was kept in a dungeon without food or water for a week. At that time, he composed some very pathetic songs to Sri Rama asking Him why, after following His orders, he was suffering like this. He was about to commit suicide, when the emperor was awakened one night by two men claiming to be servants of Ramdas. They presented the emperor with a bag of gold coins equal to the amount which Ramdas had usurped and requested the emperor to release Ramdas.

Ramdas was released, and when the coins were examined, they were found to bear the image of Sri Rama on the front and Hanuman on the back, with the imprint of some undecipherable letters. Realizing that he had seen the Lord, the king sent Ramdas back to Bhadrachalam in honor and every year sent a large gift of gold to the temple for the celebration of an annual festival. I saw one of the coins which Sri Rama had given to the emperor. All but two of them had disappeared over the years. I also saw the temple treasury, which contained many precious gem inlaid crowns and other gold ornaments which had been presented by the emperor every year as long as he lived.

It seems that Ramdas had a subsequent dream, in which Sri Rama told him that because, in his previous life, he had kept a parrot imprisoned in a cage for a week, so in his present life he had to be likewise imprisoned. The emperor had been a king greatly devoted to God and had performed a special worship of the Lord Siva by personally carrying a thousand pots of water from a river and pouring it on the image in the temple. Due to exhaustion and irritation, he threw the thousandth pot of water on the image instead of pouring it, and because of that he had to take another birth but could have the Vision of God in a personal form due to his previous devotion. Judging from the sanctity of the atmosphere there, the story is no doubt true. Swamiji and Ratnamji both enjoyed continuous Divine Bliss for the whole week.

Unfortunately, due to the strain, Ratnamji had a relapse of the tuberculosis, and started running a high fever. He and I took the first train to Arunachala after the festival was over. His condition quickly worsened, the disease having gone into his brain cavity, causing an unbearable head-ache. What was worse was that the previous medicine had no effect.

Being at a loss to know what to do, I went to the Tomb of Ramana and prayed for guidance. After that, I felt that I should find the European doctor who had initially discou-raged me from associating with Ratnamji. On seeing me, he asked why Ratnamji was not to be seen nowadays. I told him about his condition. He immediately came with me to the house and examined Ratnamji. He gave me a supply of strong pain killer and immediately wrote to another ashram where he had seen a supply of a foreign drug which would bring the disease under control. Within a few days, the medicine arrived and Ratnamji was soon improving.

The doctor told him that if he did not take three months bed rest, he would certainly suffer another relapse, and it would be very difficult to bring it under control. As it was, he had become immune to the drugs previously used. Even though Ratnamji was willing to follow the doctor's advice, it seemed that the Divine Will was otherwise. An event was soon to take place which would mean more exertion and another relapse. It seemed that there would be no end to Ratnamji's sufferings.

"Swamiji has written a letter to me. He says that he wants to come here and walk around the Arunachala Hill 108 times as an act of worship. That will take him at least 100 days if he goes around it once a day. You know that the distance is about eight miles and his health is not good. I also will have to accompany him. It looks as if God has some other plan for me than taking bed rest," Ratnamji said one day, smiling at me. My heart pained to hear this news. Although I was happy to hear that Swamiji would be com-ing, it meant further strain and relapse for Ratnamji. As far as he was concerned, it was all the sweet will of Ramana taking him beyond identification with the body in this painful way.

Swamiji soon arrived, along with two devotees who would look after his needs. I tried to look happy to see him, but I guess he wondered at my half-hearted expression of joy. In truth, I felt as if the messenger of death had arrived. What could I do? Ratnamji was, of course, better at making a show of happiness than I was, or perhaps he simply did not think of it at all. He seemed to be genuinely happy to see Swamiji. They spent the day talking, but Ratnamji was careful not to mention what the doctor had said about taking a rest. He did not want to spoil Swamiji's stay.

The next day, Swamiji started his circumambulation of the hill. Ratnamji also went along supported on my shoulder. He was exhausted by the time we returned. When I checked to see if he had a fever, I was surprised to find that his temperature was normal. Perhaps God would protect him, I thought.

The next day, his pace was even slower. Because of this, Swamiji was forced to slow down his own pace. Upon reaching home, I took his temperature and was sorry to find that he was running a high fever. Relapse had set in again as predicted by the doctor. I was forbidden to say anything to Swamiji about it.

The next day Swamiji came to Ratnamji and asked him not to come for the walk anymore, as it would be too much of a strain on him which also meant that Swamiji must walk at a very slow pace. Thank God! But what was the use? The damage had already been done. I went to the doctor, but he refused to come to see Ratnamji as a matter of principle. He advised a certain discipline, and we were not ready to follow it. In the future we might do the same thing again. Why should he spend his time and energy to no avail? I could not blame him for his attitude and came away wondering what to do. He suggested that we try to get the medicine through someone else. We knew two people who were in America, one of whom was my mother. I decided to write to her.

One of the people who had accompanied Swamiji to our place was a exemplary Sanskrit scholar. Ratnamji told me that, as he was unable to sit up for long, he found that reading was very difficult. His favorite book was the *Srimad Bhagavatam*, the life story of Sri Krishna in Sanskrit. It contains about 18,000 verses and takes about 10 days of continuous reading to complete. He thought that if we could get the scholar to read the book aloud, I could tape record it and he could listen to it whenever he liked. Swamiji also like the idea. My mother had brought a very costly foreign tape recorder with her when she had come to India for my house-opening ceremony and had left it with me. We decided to start recording immediately. Either before or after the daily reading, Swamiji would go around the hill as usual.

After two days of recording, something went wrong with the tape recorder. The tracks were overlapping each other. I told Ratnamji and Swamiji about it.

"Can you get it repaired here?" Ratnamji asked.

"I doubt it. It is such a costly machine. Where can we go to get it repaired? The people may destroy it instead of repairing it," I replied.

"It came from America, didn't it? Can it be repaired there? he asked.

"I am sure it can but please do not ask me to go there. Of course, if there is no other way, I am ready to do as you say," I replied.

"I know that you never want to return to America. It would be wrong of me to ask you to go. You know what the situation is. You must decide what should be done," Ratnamji concluded.

That night when I lay down to sleep, I prayed to Ramana to show me what I should do. As soon as I fell asleep, I had a vivid dream. I saw my mother standing in front of me and by my side were Ratnamji and Swamiji. They were both pointing at her feet. I understood what they intended and went and prostrated to her and touched her feet. As soon as I touched her, I woke up. I woke up Ratnamji, and told him about the dream. He did not say anything. I said that I thought that Ramana had showed me that I should go to America. But where was I to get the money for the tickets? He told me to go back to sleep, that we would see in the morning. The next morning when Swamiji came into the room, Ratnamji told him about my dream.

"You know, some devotees want me to conduct a festival here just like the one we did in Bhadrachalam. In fact, they have already given me some money so that the initial arrangements can be made. You take it, go to America, and come back as soon as possible. We shall look after Ratnamji until you return, but do not delay," Swamiji said.

That morning after breakfast, I took leave of them and

hurried to Madras. There just happened to be a vacant seat on the night flight to New York. I did not even have time to inform my mother that I would be coming. What if she were not in town when I arrived? Hoping for the best, I took the ticket and boarded the plane that night. Twenty-four hours later found me in New York. I felt as if I were dreaming. America and India are two completely different worlds. It had been six or seven years since I had left America, and during those years, I had lead the life of a traditional Hindu monk. I had not even changed my dress but traveled in my dhoti with a shawl covering the upper half of my body. Even shoes were absent! I felt like a small baby pushed out from the warmth and comfort of the house into a street lined with skyscrapers. I thought that I had better call my mother in Chicago and make sure that she was there.

"Hello, Mother?"

"Who is this?" she asked.

"Why, who else but me?" I replied.

"Neal? Where are you? Your voice is so clear! What is the matter?" she exclaimed.

"I am in New York at the airport. I am waiting for the flight to Chicago. Can you meet me at the airport there? I will explain everything later."

I was waitlisted on the Chicago flight and given the last seat in the plane. Mother met me at the airport, overjoyed to see me but worried that I was sick. I explained everything to her and told her that I must return immediately, tomorrow if possible. She did not like the idea of my going so soon but agreed to do what was necessary. That same day, we took the tape recorder to a shop, but as it was Friday, and we were told we could not pick it up until Monday. I asked my mother to reserve my return ticket for Tuesday. I think she was in a state of shock similar to the way I was feeling or she would not have agreed so easily. I told her that I had a very poor friend in India who needed a certain costly drug for the treatment of tuberculosis which is not available in India. I asked if she could procure it. I did not tell her that the poor friend was Ratnamji, or she would have worried that I would catch tuberculosis. We contacted the family doctor and were told that it would take a few days to get the drug. Mother agreed to send it by airmail as soon as she got it.

Tuesday saw me in the plane back to India with a tearful mother standing in the airport. It was like a dream for both of us. After another 24 hours, I was back in Madras six days after leaving. On reaching our house, I entered and bowed down to Swamiji and Ratnamji. They smiled and asked me about my journey. I thought that they would be happy to see me, but they were their usual evenminded selves. The recording was again taken up and completed within a week.

One day I felt that I was getting no time to study or meditate. In fact, because I had to serve Ratnamji who was bedridden, I had practically no time to myself. When I tried not to think about myself, I enjoyed a reflection of the Bliss of selfless existence, but at times, I felt that I should live alone somewhere and devote some time to spiritual discipline. Because of such thoughts, I became half-hearted in serving Ratnamji. It did not take Swamiji long to notice this and he called me aside one day.

"Child, why are you attending to your duties in such a half-hearted way?" he asked. "Is it because you want to go away and practice meditation by yourself? I also felt like that at one time. You will always be able to find plenty of time for such things, but to have the company of a real sage and be allowed to have a close relationship with him is extremely rare. People are searching all over the world for a real saint but cannot find one. Both of us are sick and may not stay in this world much longer. Though we do not depend upon your serving us, you ought to think over what you should do. Which way lies your duty? If you want to go away and do intensive meditation, we have no objection, but if you decide to stay on, you should work with your whole mind and heart. Only then you will get the benefit of serving saints. You must decide for yourself."

I already knew that what Swamiji was saying was true, and I told him that in the future I would do full justice to my chosen path of serving the sages. If meditation in solitude was necessary for me, I would do it when their company was no longer available.

After completing his vow of 108 circumambulation of the holy Arunachala Hill, Swamiji arranged the festival as planned. Nearly 500 people from different parts of India attended the function, which lasted for a week. After this, Swamiji decided to go north and presented Ratnamji with some money to be used for purchasing medicines. Ratnamji had been suffering all these days with 101 degree fever but did not let Swamiji know about it. Now that Swamiji was going, we also planned to leave to find a good doctor and get treatment. The day after Swamiji left, we packed our things and intended to start the next day. I had put the money in a cupboard in my house, where Ratnamji's sister was sleeping. Ratnamji and I were sleeping in his house. Suddenly at 1:00 a.m. Ratnamji called me.

"Get up and go to the other house. I feel as if some theft is taking place. Hurry!" he said.

When I went to the other house, I found that the door was locked from the outside. I opened it. Seshamma was fast asleep, and the money was missing from the cupboard. The thieves had removed the cement slab covering the chimney and had lowered themselves into the house. After taking what they wanted, they quietly went out, locking the door behind them.

In the morning, the police were called and a police dog was brought from Madras. The dog caught a man who was working in a nearby house, the brother of our gardener. The man was taken into custody by the police, but someone used influence to have him released, and that was the end of the matter. As we had no more money, we had to wait until some friends could send us enough for our journey and doctor's fees.

A few days later, I had a dream that I saw Swamiji's dead body being pulled this way and that by various people. I mentioned this to Ratnamji, but he simply nodded, not making any comment. Shortly after this, we received word that Swamiji had suddenly died of a heart attack in Hyderabad. In fact, there was a tug of war over his body. Only after a letter he had written many years earlier was found, stating that after death he wanted his body immersed in the Krishna River in South India, did the bickering stop.

We reached the banks of the Krishna River as soon as we could and found that the funeral rites had not yet started. For the next 15 days, Ratnamji took charge of the situation and made sure that all of the prescribed rituals were performed perfectly. This required continuous supervision on his part and the strain caused his health to deteriorate still further. He seemed to be a blazing light in a broken container. He was determined to do what he felt was his duty, even at the cost of his life, and God was certainly giving him opportunities one after another to do so.

I breathed a sigh of relief when the ceremonies were at last over and we could go to a doctor. The doctor prescribed various herbs and minerals to be taken with honey or butter and told us that, in his opinion, Ratnamji was not suffering from tuberculosis but rather from a chronic type of bronchitis. He told Ratnamji to return home and take the medicines for a few months.

Before we left for Arunachala, some friends consulted an astrologer concerning Ratnamji's future. They were told that he would not live more than nine months. After hearing this news, Ratnamji decided to make out a will. He left his house and library to me. Those were the only possessions that he had. He felt that I would use them as he would have.

In Tiruvannamalai, Ratnamji set to work arranging his library of nearly 2,000 rare books. It had taken him nearly 35 years to collect these volumes. Wherever he went during his travels, he purchased a book if money was available. Now he felt that they should be arranged in proper order, so that I would not have to struggle to arrange them afterwards. He also read the *Garuda Purana,* an ancient book which is concerned with the last rites of departed souls and describes the post-death journey to the next plane of existence. Taking notes, he translated them into English and made me study them, so that I would be able to supervise his last ceremonies as he had done for Swamiji. Finally, he even made out a list of the people who should be informed about his passing. In fact, the only thing he left for me to do was to fill in the date of demise!

"Why are you doing all this?" I asked him one day. "I will somehow manage. I cannot bear to see all these things being done by you. Who knows, maybe you will get better and live another 50 or 60 years!"

"Even if I live another 100 years, I must leave the body

someday. At that time, are you going to be able to think of all of these things? This is simply a rehearsal, so that you don't worry when the time comes and things will be done properly. You know, everybody celebrates their children's marriages or the birth of a baby or similar functions. Being a lifelong bachelor, this is the only celebration that I have. Let it be done in a grand way. My body will be an offering to the god of death. You could say that this will be the final oblation," Ratnamji laughingly said.

During the next six or seven months Ratnamji continued to take the herbal treatment, which did not seem to make him either worse or better. His sister Seshamma invited him to her village to take part in a special worship she and her husband were conducting there. They wanted his presence and supervision. We fixed a date for the journey and made the necessary preparations. He asked me to go and collect a few books from a friend of his in the ashram who had borrowed them some months back. The friend was an old gentleman who had an intuitive gift for telling the future. He asked me where we would be going and when we would return. I told him about our program.

"Tell Ratnamji to finish everything before the 21st of February." he said. "Something may happen around that time. Also, I feel that you are going to have to take a loan for one year for the benefit of someone dear to you." A loan? I could not imagine what he was talking about. I returned to Ratnamji and conveyed the message.

After reaching Seshamma's village, Ratnamji began preparations for the worship. It was to be a very big affair involving many hours of worship, giving gifts, and feeding guests. The preparations took nearly three weeks. He insisted that only the best materials be used and would send back anything not up to the mark. Gradually, his health was improving. The fever and phlegm in his lungs had subsided. Perhaps the herbal doctor was right after all.

At last the day for the puja arrived. It started at 6 in the morning and was completed only at midnight, 18 hours in all! Ratnamji sat for the whole thing and supervised every detail. He did not get up even to go for nature calls and did not eat or drink anything until it was all over. I was afraid of what would happen to his body, but he was in another plane altogether, not concerned for life or for death. His body gave off a visible glow which attracted even small children. It was so conspicuous that all the villagers questioned him as to what such a Divine glow could be.

"I did not know," he replied simply. "Perhaps it is a manifestation of my Guru's blessings." In fact, it was the effulgence born of his Self Realization which could not be hidden.

One day about two weeks after the completion of the special worship, Ratnamji called me to his side.

"I am feeling much better now," he said. "After a few days we can return to Arunachala. Even so, I feel that I will leave my body this month or else after six months." As he was saying this, his left leg started to shake uncontrollably. I caught hold of it with my hands. The other leg also started to shake, and I somehow managed to catch that also. When I looked at his face, I saw that his arms were also shaking and he was starting to go into what seemed to be an epileptic fit. I rushed into the kitchen and called his nephew to come and help me. By the time we returned to his bedside, we found that he had become unconscious. Within 20 minutes, he regained consciousness, but before he could say anything, another fit set in and made him unconscious. This occurred every 20 minutes. We sent for the doctor, who arrived shortly and tried to administer some medicine, but it was difficult to get Ratnamji to swallow it. After the third or fourth fit, he said only a few words, "This is all your kindness, oh God!"

He never spoke another word. The fits continued every 20 minutes. Gradually, his body was getting weaker and weaker, and the severity of the fits was lessening due to the weakness of his body. I arranged a number a people to sit around his bed chanting the Divine Name. It was obvious that the time for his departure was near. Strangely enough, I did not feel the least bit worried or afraid. I felt that the whole scene going on before me was a drama and that I must simply play my part. Finally, at 2:30 a.m., on the 18th of February, Ratnamji breathed his last. He opened his eyes and smiled and was no more. The look of perfect peace and inner Bliss in his eyes made me think that he was in Samadhi. His body was carried out of the house and placed in a shed in the yard where well-wishers could pay their last respects.

Singing of the Divine Name continued throughout the night and the next day until the evening, when the body was bathed and taken to the cremation grounds on the outskirts of the village. I came along to make sure that everything was done properly, as he had wished. Many hundreds of people came from the surrounding villages to see the body of a great saint before it was offered into the flames. After the funeral pyre was lit, everyone went home. Only a friend and I remained in the cremation grounds near the burning pyre to make sure that no dogs would try to eat the body or disturb the pyre.

I felt a mixture of joy and sorrow at the same time. Ratnamji had at last been released from the painful cage of his body after a life of spiritual endeavor. His soul had gone to his Guru Ramana. At the same time, I was left behind to fend for myself. He had been my all in all for the past eight years. He had taught me everything from about spiritual life. Now he was gone. But was he? I clearly felt his presence within me as the light of awareness. During the coming days, I experienced a peculiar sense of identification with him. Although I did not know whether others could perceive it, I felt as if my facial expressions became like his, as well as my way of speaking, and even my way of thinking. I felt as if my body and personality were just a shadow of his. Though separated from him physically, I was enjoying a deep peace within. I suppose it was a surprise for everybody to see me like that. Because I was like his own son for eight years, others thought that I would be irreconcilably miserable at his passing. They were surprised to see that, if anything, I was more happy. Was this not due to his Blessings? I felt so.

According to the Hindu Scriptures, after death the soul does not immediately proceed to the other world. It requires some sort of body with which to make the journey. Usually, a small stone is placed on the corpse at the time of cremation. After the fire has subsided, this stone and some of the remaining bone chips are recovered. For 10 days, food is cooked and offered with appropriate mantras to the deceased, using the stone as a medium. It is believed that each day the food is offered, a part of the body needed for travel in the subtle realm is formed. For example, the first day's offering goes to make up the feet, the second day's to make up the calves, and so on. The offering is called a pinda, and the body which is formed from the subtle essence of the food is called pinda sariram, sariram meaning a body. On the tenth day, the soul becomes conscious of its surroundings and the existence of the pinda sariram. It comes to the place where it's well-wishers are gathered for the ceremonies and sees who has come. Afterwards, it starts on its journey to the next world.

These ceremonies were all conducted for Ratnamji. On the tenth day, the stone having fulfilled its purpose was cast into the river nearby. It happened to be the same river in which Swamiji's body had been immersed nine months earlier. That day happened to be Sivaratri, an annual festival which is celebrated throughout India. On that day, people fast and stay awake the whole night worshipping God until the dawn breaks.

Exhausted from the ceremonies and not in a very happy mood, I lay down to sleep at about 11:00 at night. Immediately, Ratnamji appeared in a vivid dream. He smiled and held out his hand. I looked at it and found that the stone was resting in his palm. He then threw it into the river and told me, "Come, tonight is Sivaratri. We must worship the Lord." He then sat down, and asking me to sit next to him, started the puja.

I abruptly awoke and had the certain feeling that what I had just seen was not a mere dream, but that Ratnamji had wanted to show me that he was still very much alive and with me, though in a subtle form unseen by me. I felt extremely happy and could hardly sleep the rest of the night.

Chapter V

FENDING FOR MYSELF

After the completion of the ceremonies, I took Ratnamji's few possessions with me and returned to Arunachala. I had after all come to Arunachala eight years ago to live near the tomb of Ramana and to try to attain Realization of my True Nature. I felt that I had been guided these past eight years by Ramana in the form of Ratnamji. Now I must put into practice all that had been learned. The foundation had been laid. Now the building must be raised.

On the train on the way back, I had another wonderful dream. I found that I had arrived at the ashram and there was a big crowd assembled at the foot of the hill. I came closer and saw that Ramana's body lay there unmoving. He had died just a short while back. Everyone was weeping. I came near his body and started to weep, "Oh Ramana, I have come all this way to see you, but before I could reach you, you left!" Then Ramana opened his eyes and smiled at me. He asked me to sit down and placed his feet in my lap and asked me to press his legs.

"They say I am dead. Do I look dead to you?" he asked. I then woke up and wondered at the clarity of the dream. Surely Ramana was with me. I became convinced of this.

Our houses seemed empty and devoid of life without Ratnamji. I wondered how I would be able to stay in his house without him. I felt that he was within me, but there was no doubt that he was physically absent. The Bliss which I had felt continuously in his company was no longer there. I decided to meet with the astrologer in the ashram. He welcomed me and asked me about Ratnamji. I told him everything. I also told him that not only was he correct in predicting that Ratnamji should finish his work before the 21st of February, but also that I had needed to ask my mother for a loan in order to perform the monthly ceremonies for the departed which are done for one year following the death. I told him I was surprised at the accuracy of his predictions.

"Would you tell me what the future holds for me now that Ratnamji is gone?" I asked.

"Your health will gradually deteriorate," he began, "and after four years there is a chance that you will die. If not, you will go to your mother and continue your spiritual life. At the same time, you will be busy collecting money."

Death? Going back to America? Collecting money? It all sounded too terrible to be true. I thanked him and went back to the house. I started to worry. I knew this man's words could not be false, and I felt very sad and restless. There was nobody I could talk to about it. For 10 days, I brooded over the matter, unable to meditate or even read anything. This probably would have continued but for a dream I had. Ratnamji was standing in the house looking at me with an expression of irritation on his face.

"Why are you acting like this?" he said. "Everything is in Ramana's hands. You have surrendered your life to him, have you not? You must do your duty by meditating on God day and night. What is to happen to you will be looked after by Ramana. Do not worry." I woke up. Not a trace of drowsiness remained,and I felt relieved of a burden. From that time onwards, thoughts of the future ceased to plague me.

During the next year, I decided to travel to Hyderabad to take part in the monthly ceremonies to be performed for Ratnamji's soul. On one occasion, after finishing the meal and lying down for rest in the house of the man who had performed the rituals, I dreamt that Ratnamji and Ramana were standing next to each other and looking at me. Ramana pointed at Ratnamji and said to me, "By serving him, you are serving me." Though I call these experiences dreams, I must make it clear that they did not have the hazy quality of a dream. They were almost as clear as the waking consciousness but with some peculiarity of their own; I felt I was neither awake nor dreaming. They left a deep impression on me that I was being looked after and guided by these great men.

About six months after Ratnamji's passing, my mother decided to come to India with my sister and brother-in-law. We traveled for about 10 days in Kashmir, one of the most picturesque parts of India. From there, we flew to eastern India and stayed at Darjeeling, a hill station famous for its tea estates, where one has magnificent views of Mount Everest and Kanchenjunga. As we drove up the hills from the plains, I started to feel overjoyed for no apparent reason. I actually started to roll in laughter. No one could make out what was so funny, nor could I myself explain it. I did have the feeling that there must be a great number of holy men living in that area whose very presence was making me feel so Blissful.

That night when I lay down to sleep, Ratnamji appeared to me. He looked at me as if waiting for me to say something. I ventured to ask him, "Ratnamji, when you died, what happened to you at that moment?" I had seen that he looked as if he was in Samadhi, or perfect union with God.

He replied, "At that moment, I felt a force rising up from within and overwhelming me. I surrendered to it and was merged into that." He then turned away, walked into the sky, and gradually disappeared.

Upon completion of the year of monthly ceremonies for Ratnamji's soul, I decided to remain in Arunachala for the coming year. I requested all of my friends not to come there. I wanted to spend that year in complete seclusion, meditating and studying, trying to assimilate the experiences of the past nine years. I started to have serious doubt as to what should be my main spiritual practice. According to Ramana, there are only two main paths, the Path of Devotion to God characterized by the incessant repetition of the Divine Name or a mantra, and the Path of Knowledge characterized by ceaseless inquiring into oneself as to what it is that shines as "I."

Ratnamji had advised me to walk in the Path of Devotion for the first six years that we were together. Then, he called me one day and told me that I must take up Self-inquiry more and more, as only that would purify my mind enough to render it unmoving and fit for absorption into the Real. He made me spend several hours every day in a room meditating on my innermost Self. Now the doubt came to me as to what should be my practice. I felt that the Path of Knowledge was creating in me a subtle sort of false pride. Though seeing a reflection of the Truth within, I was still a far distance from realizing that Truth to be my Real Self. I thought that to be a humble devotee of God or Guru would be a safer way, but Ratnamji's words should also be taken into consideration.

I spent many days vacillating between the two choices. Then one night, I had another significant dream. A realized sage, the Shankaracharya of Kanchipuram, whom I held in high reverence, appeared sitting before me. He said, "May I enter into Thee. May I enter into Thee. Repeat this every day for nine hours." I requested him to repeat the same verse in Sanskrit. "This is enough!" he said somewhat angrily, and I woke up. From the next day, I tried to repeat the verse for nine hours. I felt very awkward repeating those words, so I repeated my own mantra with those words in my mind. My body was already becoming weaker day by day, and I found it impossible to sit up for so many hours. I somehow managed to do this repetition for five hours every day. By the end of each day, I felt a very definite effect in the form of a deepening of inner peace. I went on like this for two or three months.

Then one day the Acharya again appeared to me in a dream. He was seated before me, just as in the previous dream.

"The mind alone is important," he said. He then offered me a banana leaf containing a mound of sugar candy. He took a piece himself, put it into his mouth, and got up and walked away. From the next day, I had no inclination to sit for repetition of the mantra. I found that Self inquiry came about very easily, and so I started to take up that practice with all seriousness. It dawned on me what he had meant by "the mind alone is important." It is not which spiritual practice you do that is important, but rather the purity of mind which is gained thereby. One should have an eye to that only. The practices are only means to an end.

At the end of two years, when it was time to perform the second annual ceremony for Ratnamji, the devotees in Hyderabad expressed a wish that the rituals be done in Benaras, or Kasi as it is called. By that time I was feeling too weak to travel. I had extreme pain in the lower portion of my back as well as the abdomen. All along the spine there was pain, and I had frequent migraine headaches. I was taking treatment from the government hospital in the town but did not notice any improvement. On hearing their proposal, I thought "Well, Ratnamji neglected his body in favor of attending spiritual programs. As his son, should I not do the same?"

Thinking so, I started for Hyderabad. Soon after I reached there, eight of us proceeded to Kasi and arrived there after two days. I felt very happy to be back in Kasi after a 10 year absence, but I could hardly walk or sit up. I could only lie in a corner all of the time. The night before the ceremony, I had a thrilling dream. I found myself at the foot of a hillock. I climbed up and found a small cottage inside of which was seated Ratnamji. He was glowing with a heavenly splendor, and even the house was irradiated by his presence.

"Ah, you have come all this way just to attend the ceremony? You are suffering much, are not you? I am happy to see your devotion. Here, take this and eat." Saying this he handed me a sweet cake, and I woke up in tears. He was indeed seeing all that was going on and understood my heart, just as when he was alive in the body.

With some difficulty, I returned to Arunachala. The astrologer had said that I might die within four years. Now two years were over. I had two desires that I very much wanted to fulfill before leaving the earthly plane. One was to walk around the Arunachala Hill 108 times. The other was to walk to all of the important shrines in the Himalayan region. I was too weak to do either, but I decided to try. After all, the worst that would happen is that my body would expire before its time. Let it die doing a holy act was my thought.

I slowly walked up to the tomb of Ramana in the ashram and stood there mentally asking him to give me enough strength to fulfill my desire. I felt a surge of strength and somehow was able to walk the eight miles around Arunachala Hill that day. I decided to rest on alternate days. Each time I walked up to the ashram, I felt so weak that I thought it would be impossible to walk even a few more steps. After standing in front of Ramana's shrine, however,

I found enough strength to walk around the Hill. This went on until I completed the 108 circumambulations.

Now came the time to try to fulfill the second desire. I took a train to Hyderabad and then to Kasi. My idea was to stay in Kasi for a few days and then start to walk to the Himalayas. I thought that it would take me about six months to complete the journey at a leisurely walk. Unfortunately, in Kasi I became so sick that I concluded that I could not possibly fulfill my aspiration. Admitting defeat, I retraced my steps and took a train to Hyderabad. There, I entered a nature cure hospital. I had the faith that, if anyone could diagnose and cure me, it would most probably be those whose medical systems were along the lines of naturopathy, homeopathy, or ayurveda (herbal treatment).

I stayed for two months in the hospital. The atmosphere was like an ashram with classes on Yoga, devotional singing, and various dietetic regimens. However, I continued to weaken and finally decided to seek another way. I then went to a renowned homeopath who was at that time serving the President of India. He treated me freely for two or three months, but there was no improvement. What next? A devotee friend of mine suggested that I go to America to improve my health for the sake of my spiritual life. He did not think this would harm me spiritually as I had felt all these years. He said that if I should not improve even there, I should return to India immediately.

Only one who has lived in India for some years could understand my dislike and fear of living in America. Living in India, it is very easy to discipline one's life and spend one's time in meditation, study, and other spiritual practices. There is very little to distract one. The culture itself is conducive to such a way of life.

Such is not the case in America. The American ideal being comfort and enjoyment, in whatever direction one turns, one is confronted with opportunities to forget one's spiritual goal and become immersed in pleasures. It is not human nature to seek peace of mind through renunciation of the outer by turning within to seek the inner Reality. Rather, people tend to seek happiness outside in the objects of the world. Without exception, they meet with varying amounts of disillusionment in their external search for peace, and some of them start to look within as an alternative. Having heard that there is a higher, more refined, happiness than that which the world has to offer, many take up a life dedicated to the achievement of spiritual Realization, and the resultant Infinite Bliss that can be achieved. But the old tendency to seek happiness externally somehow raises its head again and again. For this reason, it has been found that a conducive atmosphere is necessary for one walking along the razor-edged path of Self-Realization.

To demonstrate how worldly tendencies interfere with turning the mind inwards to see the Light, a story is told in India. There was once a cat who somehow got tired of chasing mice for a living. He thought that if he could learn to read he might get a better job. One night he was sitting by a candle studying the alphabet. Just then a mouse ran by. Immediately throwing aside the book and extinguishing the light, the cat jumped on the mouse! Where did his desire for reading go? Feeling myself to be much like the cat in the story, I was sure that if I spent any time in America, I would once again start running after the sensual life and would gradually lose the Inner Light I had gained through much struggle.

Deciding to give it a six-month trial, I phoned my mother that I would be coming within a few days and booked my ticket. Returning to Arunachala I went before Ramana's tomb and prayed for guidance and a safe return. Then, proceeding to Madras, I flew via Bombay to New York, where my mother came to meet me. From there she took me to her new home in Santa Fe, where she had recently moved. All the while, I maintained the attitude of a child in the hands of its mother. I decided to obey my mother strictly as a representation of God for six months. It was to be another practice in surrender to His will.

I spent the next six months going to various doctors. First, of course, I tried the allopathic system. Though the doctor was ready to admit that I was in pain and was very weak, he could not make out any cause. No diagnosis meant no treatment. Next came herbal treatment, then homeopathy coupled with a special diet. Then followed acupuncture and even hypnosis. Nothing seemed to do any good. Finally, my mother felt that I should go to a psychiatrist. I had to smile at the idea. All right, if it is your will, Ramana, I will go, I thought to myself.

"Do you remember your father?" the psychiatrist asked me.

"Of course, every minute of my life I am remembering my Father," I replied.

"Is that so? How interesting! Why would you want to remember your father so frequently? You must have had a very traumatic experience with him," he said.

"Yes, traumatic would be a good word for it. He put the desire in my mind to see Him and to become one with Him. From that day onwards I have tried to remember Him always and to see Him in all that meets my eye."

"Just what do you mean by 'father'?" he asked.

"You and I and everyone else have only one Father, that is God. We are all His children. You may not choose to believe in His existence, and that is up to you. As for myself, I cannot deny His existence. I can clearly feel His Presence within me. You may call it a mental delusion or whatever you like. I would, on the other hand, say that to feel the Real within is quite normal, and to feel nothing but thoughts and restlessness as most people do is a kind of sickness," I replied. "Even though my body is sick, I feel perfectly at peace and happy."

"You may be at peace, and so it may be all right for you, but I have many patients coming here with severe mental problems. Belief in God is no solution for them. They will ask, 'If there is a God, why this suffering?' Not only would I have no answer for them but I myself also wonder about this."

"Doctor," I began, "you were brought up in a society where Christianity and Judaism predominate. It is difficult to prove to a rationalist the existence of God or the value of surrender to His will using the tenets or philosophy of those religions. It would be only a matter of faith or blind belief. Nowadays many people think a thing over deeply before accepting it as true.

If one were to explore the philosophical side of the oriental religions, one would find them to be based on conclusions drawn from logical, methodical experiments. The conclusions drawn by the Indian sages were the fruits of their lifelong spiritual practices which gave them certain experiences. If anyone should follow the paths laid down by them, he would have the experiences that thousands have had. Their philosophy of life is perfectly logical and in accordance with present-day scientific findings.

"The highest Hindu conception of God, for example, is not that He is someone sitting in Heaven lording over creation like a dictator. Rather, the Supreme God is one's innermost core who can be directly experienced when one controls the mind and makes it subtle and peaceful. The sun cannot be clearly seen on the surface of a lake which is agitated by waves. Our mind is like a lake which, if made serene, will reflect the Divine Presence. Losing sight of the gem which is within us, we run restlessly around in search of happiness. We cannot sit still even for a minute. The moment we enjoy some object, our mind becomes quiet for a short time, and that quietude we call happiness. It follows logically that, if one controls the risings of the mind and makes it quiet in itself without using enjoyment as a means, happiness becomes a continuous experience.

"In the east, religion is not merely a matter of faith, but rather it is the science of controlling the mind to obtain the direct experience of Reality, which is the source of the mind. Actions which take us away from that Center within could be called bad. God is that which takes one nearer to the Center. The science of physics states that every action has an equal and opposite reaction. This applies to all spheres of life, physical as well as mental. As one sows, so must one reap. If we do harm physically or mentally to others, we must ultimately suffer the same harm. This holds true for doing good to others. The fruit may not come immediately, but come it must, if science is correct.

"This, of course, necessitates the belief in a previous and a future existence, for otherwise, why do we suffer for something which we cannot remember having done or why do we experience enjoyment for no merit of our own? Some people lead very wicked lives and escape unhurt; others do only good to others and suffer their whole lives. What one is experiencing in this life is, to a large extent, due to the actions in a previous life. No one comes with a clean slate. What we do today will come back to us tomorrow or in some future birth. We are the makers of our own destiny and cannot blame God for our sufferings. To balance the accounts is Nature's Law. It is for us to learn those laws and live in harmony with them to avoid suffering and to attain eternal peace and happiness.

"If one keeps in mind that, while reaping the fruits of one's actions in the form of pleasant or painful experiences, one is only clearing one's account, then the mind will remain peaceful and not become either miserable or overjoyed. In such a peaceful mind the extremely subtle Light which is the very Source of the mind and its occasional flashes of happiness, will be clearly seen and entered into. That is the essence of Bliss, and such a one is henceforth called a sage and shines forth as a source of inspiration to erring humanity.

"Though you might be able to pacify your patients and resolve some of their problems, new problems will come up again and again. Only if one understands that the mind itself can be controlled and made free from all thoughts including the troublesome ones, will it be possible to advise a person properly so that problems cease to arise, at least on the mental plane. I do not know if you could follow all that I just said. It may seem to you to be a strange way of looking at things."

The psychiatrist did, in fact, understand what I had said, for he had studied a bit of Indian philosophy. He had also felt that tackling the mind itself instead of each of its numberless problems was a more logical way of attaining peace, but as he had no training in how to do it, he could not advise anyone to do so. On leaving, I gave him a copy of a book entitled *Who Am I?*, which contains the teaching of Ramana in a very concise form. He invited me to lunch on another day, and we had a long conversation on spiritual topics. Seeing all of this, my mother came to the conclusion that I was not going to benefit from psychiatry, so she did not press me to continue the meetings. I also told her that, as far as I was concerned, there was no need to pay the psychiatrist 50 dollars a day just so I could give him some peace of mind!

It had already been five months since my return to the

United States. My departure date was nearing. The only thing that was keeping me from catching the plane was the fact that I had applied for a longer entry visa into India and the reply was late in coming. Meanwhile, a very troublesome situation was developing on another front. For the past three or four months, a girl of my age was coming regularly to see me. If she could not come one day, then she would at least call me on the phone to find out how I was faring. At first I thought that she had some interest in spiritual matters, and for that reason, she wanted to spend some time with me. I would speak only spiritual talk with her. After some time, I noticed that she was now and then making what could be interpreted as amorous gestures. I dismissed it as a figment of my impure imagination or perhaps just some aspect of female nature.

I began to feel a kind of subtle pleasure in her company, and some times I wondered how it was that I felt that the path of complete abstinence from worldly enjoyment was the path for me. I was surprised that such thoughts were coming into my mind. I knew that, even if I were to fall prey to temptation, it would only be for a moment, for I had already gone through the worldly life and had become disillusioned by it. Yet, a fall would be a fall, and time and energy would be lost. Seeing the tendency of mind I decided that I must return to India at the first possible opportunity.

I did not have to wait long. My visa came within a few days, and I booked my ticket immediately. My mother, of course, did not want me to go, but I was adamant. The day for my departure arrived. The girl came to the house to see me off. Taking me aside, she said, "Neal, must you go? I love you very much."

"I love you also but only as a brother loves a sister," I replied. "Besides, it is not possible for me to love one person more than another. The same spark is in everyone, and it is to that thing which I offer my love. Though there may be different types of machines, the current of electricity that makes them work is only one. That Thing which makes our bodies alive and attractive is one and the same in all, and as soon as it departs only a corpse remains behind. We should love only That," I replied, glad that I was on my way back to India.

Home, sweet home! I thought that I would never see you again, my beloved Mother India. Though not wealthy in material riches, you have the wealth of spiritual austerities of thousands of your children who have attained the Infinite Bliss of God Realization down through the ages. Oh Mother, let me not leave you again!

India was dear to me before I left. Now after my return, she had become doubly so. I went straight to Arunachala and tried to regain my usual mental state. I found that spending those six short months in America had indeed affected my detachment, as I had feared. Instead of taking a constant delight in meditating on the Light within, an urge to enjoy external objects and the restlessness that goes with it entered a corner of my mind. I wondered if I would ever regain my old state. However, I spent as much time as possible near Ramana's shrine, and the previous condition was soon restored.

The subtle, insidious effect of living in a worldly atmosphere became crystal clear to me. The tendency to look outward slowly steals away the hard-earned inner wealth of a life of intense meditation. If there is even a small leak in a vessel, soon one will find that all of the water has disappeared, one knows not where.

My health continued to deteriorate day by day. I could hardly walk 100 yards due to weakness, and I could not sit up for more than a few minutes. The pains in the back increased greatly, and even eating became painful. I felt as if there was an ulcer somewhere near the duodenum. On the advice of a local homeopathic doctor, I started to eat only the soft inner portion of bread and drink milk. I found even this to be painful. I wondered how many more days my body would survive like this. Death would be preferable, but that was not in my hands. I had surrendered to Ramana and had to accept the condition in which he placed me. I was taking medicines, but whether or not there would be any improvement was entirely in his hands.

At this juncture, I came across a book entitled *I Am That,* a collection of conversations with Nisargadatta Maharaj, a Realized Soul living in Bombay. I felt that his teachings were identical to Ramana's, and as I had not seen Ramana during his lifetime, I entertained a strong desire to see someone like him. Going to Bombay seemed out of the question, so I wrote a letter to Maharaj explaining my spiritual and mental condition and requested his blessings. The very next day, after I had posted the letter, a French lady came to visit me. She had read the same book recently and had decided to go to Bombay and see Maharaj. I told her of my desire and my inability to travel.

"You could take a plane to Bombay? If you like, I will help you get there," she said.

I thought that this must be a godsend, and I immediately agreed to her proposal. She had read many books on the philosophy of nondualism which states that there is only one Reality, the world being a manifestation of That, and that one's True Nature is only That. It is all but impossible to attain that consciousness without a one-pointed devotion to God or Guru and a complete purification of one's body, speech, and mind, including one's actions. Amanda, as she was called, felt as most pseudo-nondualists do, that nothing else is necessary except the superficial conviction that oneself is That. In the name of being that Supreme Truth, such people indulge in every kind of undisciplined, irresponsible, and sometimes immoral activity. While we were on the way to Madras in a taxi, she questioned me, "Why all this discipline, rules, and regulations? Even devotion to God is unnecessary. All of these things are only for weak-mindfed people. You should just go on thinking I am That, I am That, and you will realize the Truth of it one day."

"I think that you have overlooked an important point in the philosophy of nonduality," I objected. "All of the texts and teachers of that school of thought insist that, before one even takes up the study of it, one must have certain qualifications. A child in kindergarten cannot possibly do justice to a college textbook. He may even pervert the meaning. In the same way, before one takes up the study or practice of nonduality, the mind should be rendered unmoving to such an extent that the reflection of the Real can be seen therein. Holding on to that reflection leads one to the Original. If the reflection is not visible, what is one to fix his mind on in the name of oneself being the Truth. Thoughts, feelings, body? We are already doing quite a lot of mischief to this small, perishable body. If we start to think that we are the Supreme, what will we not hesitate to do? What is a demon or a dictator but one who feels his little self to be equal to or greater than God? There is not even a trace of bad in the Supreme, and one who has not given up such negative qualities as lust, anger, and greed cannot be taken as one who has realized the Truth. A safer course would be to consider oneself as a child of a Realized Soul, or of God. To benefit from being the child of such a One, we must try to approximate his character. Only if we can do this, will our minds gradually become pure and unruffled by passions and the Truth will be seen, and not until then."

"You are really weak-minded. You will see when we get to Maharaj. He will tell you to throw all this mushy sentimentalism overboard," she retorted, somewhat irritated. I had already met a number of people like her and knew there would be no value in arguing, so I kept quiet.

Reaching Bombay, a friend took us to Maharaj's apartment. Maharaj had been a dealer in cigarettes as a young man. One day a friend of his took him to see a famous holy man who was in Bombay. The holy man initiated Maharaj into a mantra and also told him to purify his mind by getting rid of all thoughts and holding on to the sense of being, or "I am," within. He tried this intensely for three years, and after many mystic experiences, found his mind merged into the Transcendent Reality. He stayed on in Bombay, doing business and instructing those who came to him in spiritual matters. He was now in his 80's and lived with his son in a three-room flat. He had also created a small loft in the living room, where he spent most of his time. It was there that we met him.

"Come in, come in. You are coming from Arunachala, are you not? Your letter came yesterday. Are you enjoying peace near Ramana?" Maharaj jovially asked me, motioning me to sit near him. Immediately I felt an intense peace near him, a sure sign that he was a great soul.

"Do you know what I mean by peace?" he asked. "When you put a donut in boiling oil a lot of bubbles will come out, until all of the moisture in the donut is gone. It also makes a lot of noise, does it not? Finally, all is silent, and the donut is ready. The silent condition of mind which comes about through a life of meditation is called peace. Meditation is like the boiling oil. It will make everything in the mind come out. Only then will peace be achieved." This was a very vivid and precise explanation of spiritual life, if I had ever heard one!

"Maharaj, I have written to you about the spiritual practices that I have done until now. Kindly tell me what more remains to be done," I requested of him.

"Child, you have done more than enough. It will be quite sufficient if you just go on repeating the Divine Name until the end is reached. Devotion to your Guru is the path for you; it should become perfect and unbroken by thoughts. Whatever may come to you, accept it as His gracious will for your good. You are hardly able to sit up, are not you? It does not matter. Some people's bodies become sick like this when they sincerely do meditation and other spiritual practices. It depends on the physical constitution of each. You should not give up your practices, but persist until you reach the goal or until the body dies," he said.

Turning to Amanda he asked, "What kind of spiritual practice are you doing?"

"I just go on thinking that I am the Supreme Being," she replied in a somewhat proud tone.

"Is that so? Did you never hear of Mira Bai? She was one of the greatest lady saints ever born in India. From her childhood, she felt that Lord Sri Krishna was her all in all and spent most of her days and nights in worshipping Him and singing songs about Him. Finally, she had a mystic vision of Him and her mind merged into Him. She thenceforth sang songs about the glory and Bliss of the God-Realized state. At the end of her life, she entered into a Krishna temple and disappeared in the sanctum sanctorum. You should walk in the same path as her if you want to achieve the goal," Maharaj said smilingly.

Amanda turned pale. Maharaj had pulverized her mountain of nonduality in one stroke! She could not speak.

"I may talk on nonduality to some of the people that come here," Maharaj continued. "That is not for you, and you should not pay any attention to what I am telling others. The book of my conversations should not be taken as the last word on my teachings. I had given answers to the

questions of certain individuals. Those answers were intended for those people and not for all people. Instruction
can be on an individual basis only. The same medicine
cannot be prescribed for all.

"Nowadays people are full of intellectual conceit. They
have no faith in the ancient traditional practices leading up
to Self-Knowledge. They want everything served to them
on a platter. The Path of Knowledge makes sense to them,
and because of that, they may want to practice it. They will
then find that it requires more concentration than they can
muster, and slowly becoming humble, they will finally take
up easier practices like repetition of a mantra or worship of
a form. Slowly, the belief in a Power greater than themselves will dawn on them, and a taste for devotion will
sprout in their heart. Then only will it be possible for them to
attain purity of mind and concentration. The conceited
have to go a very roundabout way. Therefore, I say that
devotion is good enough for you," Maharaj concluded.

It was time for lunch, so we left Maharaj to himself. As
we were leaving, he asked me if I would be staying for
some days in Bombay.

"I don't know. I have no plans," I replied.

"Very good. Then you come here this evening after
4," he said.

The evening saw me back in Maharaj's room. He
asked me to sit near him. Though I had known him only for
a few hours, I felt as if I were his own child, that he was my
mother or father. A European came and put a large curren-
cy note in front of Maharaj.

"Please take it back. I am not interested in anyone's
money. My son is there, and he is feeding me and looking
after my needs. After you attain some peace of mind, there
will be enough time for these things. Take your money,
take it!" he exclaimed.

With great difficulty I sat and watched what went on until 7 o'clock. I felt fully satisfied and peaceful and thought
that I could not possibly get anything more than Maharaj
had told me. I thought of going back to Arunachala the next
day. I mentioned it to him and asked him for his blessings.

"If you feel like that, then you may go. Do you know
what my blessing is for you? Until you leave your body,

may you have full devotion and surrender to your Guru," Maharaj looked at me compassionately. Moved at his kindness, I started to cry but controlled myself. Even then, a few tears trickled down my cheeks. He smiled and gave me a piece of fruit. He then got up and, taking a huge pair of cymbals, started to sing devotional songs in praise of his Guru. I bowed down to him and went to rest in my room. I had not seen Amanda since the morning. I thought that the humiliation must have been too much for her, and she did not want to show her face. I therefore struggled on my own and somehow reached Arunachala, minus a sadder but wiser Amanda.

Chapter VI

MAKING IT FULL

During the next few months at Arunachala, I stopped making efforts at improving my health. Maharaj had told me that the cause was of a spiritual nature. I had also heard of such things before. Ramana had once explained to a devotee that although the life force flows outwards through the senses in most people, a spiritual aspirant endeavors to turn it back and make it merge into its source which is the Supreme within oneself. This causes a strain on the nerves, somewhat like the overflowing of a dammed up river. That strain may manifest itself in a number of ways like headache, body pains, digestive troubles, heart trouble, and other symptoms. The only cure is to persist in one's practice.

Giving up the restless search for a cure resulted in much peace of mind. Remaining mostly in bed, I continued repeating my mantra as advised by Maharaj and waited to see what the future held. Let it be death or life, it was in Ramana's hands.

One night I had a very vivid dream, the last dream that I ever had of Ramana. I found myself in the ashram near the hospital there. A large crowd of devotee were milling around waiting for something. I asked what was happening and was told that Ramana had been hospitalized and may come out soon. One man came over to me and offered me a tablet for improving my health. "No thanks, I have already tried every kind of medicine and nothing helps," I told him. Just then the front door of the hospital opened, and Ramana walked out and sat down on the ground in front of the hospital in an open courtyard. I went and bowed down to him. As I was bowing, he put his hand on my head and passed it along my spine to the middle of my back. I then looked up and saw his effulgent face. He smiled and said, "Don't I know how much you are suffering? Don't worry." I then got up thinking that others may want to come near him, and at that moment woke up. Although I did not know it at that time, circumstances were soon to take a very unexpected turn.

A few days later came a knock on my door.

"May I come in?" asked the voice of a young man.

"Yes, do come in," I told him.

"Maybe you can help me. I came from Kerala. A lady there sent me here to Tiruvannamalai telling me to take a vow of silence for 41 days. She also told me to strictly avoid the company of women while here. I have tried to find accommodation on the hill in a cave, but the monk there who was occupying it talked with the townspeople mainly about this man's and that woman's love affair. I ran away and am in search of a place to stay so that I can complete my vow. Do you know of any place?" he asked.

I closely looked at him. He looked a bit what I imagined Ratnamji had looked like at that age. He was about 25 or so. He seemed to be serious about doing meditation.

"There is another house by the side of this one. It belonged to my spiritual guide. Now he is no more. You can stay there," I told him. As I had said these words, I had the sensation that I was about to burst into tears for no apparent reason. In fact, my eyes did fill up with tears, and my heart felt a sudden gush of love filling it. I could not speak for a few moments and wondered who the lady was who had sent this boy here. She must surely be a great saint. In some unknown way, her power had blessed me at the moment that I gave shelter to this child of hers. Though it may not sound very rational, that is the conclusion I came to at that moment. It later turned out to be perfectly correct.

After getting him settled in the house, I gave him something to eat. Seeing that he had no watch, I offered him a spare watch I had, so that he could know the time in order to keep up his routine. While fetching the watch, my eyes fell on a spare rosary which I thought would be useful to him and so I gave him that also.

"When I was leaving Ammachi, I asked her for a watch and a rosary. She scolded me and told me that I should ask only for the highest thing, that is, God. She also said that I would get the things needed for my practices unasked.

Now you have given me those very things," he said, obviously moved.

"Who is Ammachi?" I asked, a bit inquisitive.

"There is a small fishing village in Kerala about 30 miles north of Quilon. It is on an island with the Arabian Sea on the west and the backwaters on the east. Ammachi is the daughter of one of the villagers there. For about five or six years now, she has been curing many people of incurable diseases like cancer, paralysis, and leprosy through her spiritual power. People come to her with all kinds of worldly problems and somehow get them resolved through her blessings. Three nights a week she sits through the whole night receiving the people. At that time, she reveals her identity with Lord Krishna and the Divine Mother."

"What do you mean by that?" I interrupted. "Does she get possessed by some Divine Power at that time?"

"Well, I guess it depends upon what you want to believe. As far as I'm concerned, she is the Divine Mother Herself, but the villagers feel that Krishna comes into her and possesses her for the first half of the night and then Devi, or the Divine Mother, comes for the rest of the night. Before and after, she seems to be a completely different person and does not remember what she said at that time," he explained.

I had seen many such people over the years while traveling with Swamiji and Ratnamji. Such people are, without a doubt, channels for Divine Power, but because their minds are of varying degrees of purity, one cannot take their words as gospel truth. Their normal consciousness seems to be suspended for a time, and afterwards, they do not remember what they said or did. They do, however, derive some type of benefit from this temporary contact with the Divine in the form of intuition of varying degrees. I had lived with real sages. Why would I want to see such a person? Well, perhaps she could help me regain a bit of health, so that I need not lie in bed all day long. Thinking this, I told the young man about my condition and asked him whether Ammachi could do anything for me.

"I will write to her and hope for a reply, but only after my 41-day vow is over would it be possible for me to take you there." He then told me about some of the cases she had cured. One was a king leper who was oozing from head to foot with pus. He was more dead than alive. In fact, his brothers had already died of the same disease. His eyes, ears, and nose were hardly visible due to the devastating effect of the disease. The stench coming from his body was so much that he had to keep his begging bowl about 50 yards away from where he was standing, so that those taking pity on him could put some food in it. One day, someone told him there was a lady manifesting Divine Power in a village nearby and that maybe she would help him.

Thinking that nothing could be lost, he went there but hesitated to go near the crowd. Ammachi, who was seated in the temple as Devi, spotted him in the distance and jumping up called out to him, "Oh my son, do not worry, I am coming." She then ran to him, gave him a comforting hug, and spoke words of assurance to him. He was shaking like a leaf, afraid of what would happen to her, or for that matter, to himself. She bathed him with pots of water while he stood there with his clothes on and finally smeared handful after handful of sacred ash on his whole body. She advised him to come back every week on the three nights that she would be in the temple. She then went and changed her clothes, which had become stained with the pus from his wounds and sat the rest of the night attending on the others.

The leper came regularly for the next six weeks, and she treated him in the same way. After the sixth week, his wounds ceased to ooze and started to heal. At present, he is completely cured of the disease, although his skin bears the scars of it. If Ammachi finds even a small crack in his skin, she licks it, and it closes by the next day.

Forty-one days later found me and my new friend, Chandru, going by train to Kerala about 500 miles southwest of Arunachala. The scenery was enchanting. Kerala is considered to be the garden of India. Wherever one looks, vegetation abounds. One can find banana and coconut trees growing in every yard. The particular area where Ammachi lived was a dense forest of coconut palms too numerous to be counted, stretching for miles in all directions. It was a bit like a paradise on earth, quite in contrast to the dry, hot climate of Tiruvannamalai. Alighting from the train, we purchased some fruits and other food to give to Ammachi and took a taxi the remaining 10 miles to her village. Fortunately, Chandru was accompanying me, or else the journey would not have been possible. I was so weak that I could hardly walk a few steps.

As Chandru had not seen Ammachi for two months, I thought that he might like to spend some time alone with her without being distracted by my presence. I sat on the veranda of a nearby house and told him to go ahead and come back for me after as much time as he wanted with Ammachi. To my surprise, however, he returned within a few moments, being led by a young lady dressed in a white skirt and shirt with a white shawl over her head. I had seen only a small photo of Ammachi which had been taken some years earlier. I did not recognize her as the same person. I did, however, stand up, and Chandru said, "This is Ammachi," at which I bowed down before her. She put out her hands in order to take my hands in hers, but I hesitated. For 12 years, I had neither touched a woman nor allowed any woman to touch me. This had been part of the discipline expected of a celibate monk. Now what was I to do? I frantically looked around and spotted the fruits which I had brought for her. I placed them in her hands, relieved that I had found a solution to the problem. My relief was, however, short lived. She gave the fruits to Chandru and again stretched out her hands. Repeating the Name of God and considering her to be a saint rather than an ordinary lady, I placed my hands in hers and was led by her into the small temple where she spent most of her time. It was hardly nine feet square and had only some kind of stool or seat in the center. The walls were covered with pictures of various Hindu gods and saints. There did not seem to be any central image set up for worship. Ammachi took some vermillion powder and pressed it on the spot between my eye brows, the place where yogis say the third eye, or the eye of intuition, is located. Her hand was vibrating, or trembling, all the time. I felt a kind of intoxication but could hardly stand for more than a few minutes. I was then led to a thatched shelter near the temple where Chandru and Ammachi sat to talk. I lay down and observed her closely. She was barely five feet tall with tiny hands and feet and of dark complexion, not more than 26 or 27 years of age. I could not perceive any glow or effulgence which is usually seen radiating from the face of a great saint. In fact, her face seemed to be very affectionate to Chandru as if she were his mother.

After lying there for a few hours, I said to Chandru, "See, you are talking for a long time. It is already past noon. Don't you think that Ammachi may be hungry? In the morning, when she put her finger between my eyebrows in the temple, I felt her trembling like a person who is weak from hunger. She may be feeling very weak. Why don't you make her eat something?"

Chandru translated what I said and they both had a good laugh.

"That trembling is not due to any weakness. It is there continuously. It is due to the Power that is constantly vibrating inside her. Just note her hands closely. They are always slightly shaking like that. It has nothing to do with sickness or weakness," Chandru replied.

We then went into a house which was by the side of the temple. I was told that this is where her parents and their other children lived. It seems that she preferred to live alone in the temple or out on the sand. I was told that, even during the rainy season, one could find her sleeping or sitting in the rain quite oblivious to her body. She came and sat behind me and put her hand on the exact place on my spine where most of the pain was located.

"Son, everyone must suffer the effects of their past actions. It is due to your bad actions in your previous birth that you are suffering now. But it is all ultimately for your good only. I do not think any doctor can find the cause of this sickness. It is coming by the will of God to make you go higher in spiritual life. It would be a mistake for Mother to remove it. If you gladly bear this sickness as coming from God and cry to Him, fixing your mind on Him, then you need not take another birth. On the other hand, if Mother removes this trouble from you, you will certainly have to be born again and suffer even more than you are now," Ammachi said to me. Chandru then asked for some hot water and prepared some milk for me from milk powder and gave me some bread.

"For how long have you been eating like this?" Amma-chi asked.

"For about three months. Whatever I eat causes se-vere pain in the abdomen. Even this causes pain, but I must eat something, mustn't I?" I replied. I was accommo-dated in one room of the house on a cot there. Exhausted, I fell asleep and woke up in the middle of the night to see Chandru and Ammachi talking in the room. He again gave me something to eat, and I fell back to sleep. When I got up at 4 a.m., I found them still talking. "Doesn't she sleep?" I wondered. I later came to learn that, in fact, she would usually sleep only for two or three hours, either during the day or night, whenever convenient.

The next morning, Chandru and Ammachi came and sat near me and started to talk.

"What is the spiritual practice you are doing?" she asked.

"I am repeating the Divine Name and also doing self-inquiry. Do you feel that it is necessary to get initiated into a mantra? Is there any difference between repeating the Name of God and a mantra given by a Guru?" I asked.

"By repeating the Name of God, one can no doubt re-alize God, but initiation by a Guru will give the disciple strong faith to continue his practice with confidence that he has the power of his Guru behind him," Ammachi replied. "You have been walking in the Path of Knowledge for a long time and still have not achieved what you set out to accomplish. Why do you not try crying to God or to your Guru Ramana? You may be able to succeed in that way."

"How is it possible to cry without any reason? There should be a cause to make one cry, shouldn't there?" I questioned her.

"Is not this sickness of yours reason enough? You can hardly move and have to lie in bed all the time. You cannot even eat. You should take a photo of your Guru and, keep-ing it next to you, weep to him to reveal himself to you and rid you of all your sorrow. Just try it. It is not as impossible as you think," she told me. "I have to go to a relative's house on the other end of the island. I will come back within two or three hours." Saying this, she got up and left.

Four hours had past, and Ammachi still had not returned. I wanted to eat and asked Chandru to give me the usual milk and bread. Just as I was about to put the spoon into my mouth, I started to weep. "What is this?" I thought and put down the spoon. The weeping stopped. Again I put the spoon to my mouth; again the weeping started. I tried three or four times, but the same thing repeated itself. Chandru looked at me with a worried expression on his face.

"Is there so much pain in your stomach?" he asked.

"No, I don't know what it is. Suddenly, the image of Ammachi flashed in my mind and I started to weep like a baby. I felt a tremendous longing and restlessness to see her at that moment. Perhaps she has done something to make me feel so," I replied.

"I am going to sit out in the sun and repeat my mantra. Maybe that will make her come back sooner," Chandru said, and he went outside. I got up and went into the next room. A photo of Ammachi was hanging there. As soon as I set my eyes on it, I started to weep. I felt as if I were seeing God in the photo. The very core of my being was shaking, and my mind was fixed there. I went back and sat on the bed.

Just then Ammachi's mother came running into the room. "Ammachi is coming. We were on the other side of the backwaters and could not get a boat to take us across. Ammachi started to shout, "Chandru is sitting there in the hot sun and Neal is weeping to see me. If you do not find a boat soon, I am going to swim across the water!" Somehow, we were able to get a boat soon after that." Saying this, she looked at my tearstained face in wonder. Ammachi came into the room just then.

"Crying?" she innocently asked, as if not knowing anything. I could not raise my head and look at her. She had humbled me, and I felt as nothing before her. My mind and heart were a mere plaything in her hands. Chandru came in and narrated to her what had happened while she was gone. I had no inclination to speak and so sat silently waiting.

"Today is darshan. Many people will be coming here to see Krishna and the Divine Mother. Now the singing will start. Chandru, you show Neal where to sit when the Bhava starts." Instructing Chandru thusly, Ammachi left the room. Darshan was the audience which Ammachi was giving to the people three nights a week, and Bhava was her word for the transformation which she underwent at those times.

The singing continued for about an hour, then Ammachi got up and went into the temple. Chandru asked me to sit on the temple veranda so that I could see what was going on clearly. Ammachi then sang a song addressed to Krishna and, when she was about halfway through it, her body suddenly shook. I felt as if an invisible wave of power came out of the temple and swept over me from toe to head. My hair stood on end, and I felt full of spiritual Bliss. The heaviness of my heart which had been there due to prolonged illness vanished in a moment. Chandru came and took me into the temple.

Ammachi was standing there in the corner. She was dressed up as Krishna with a small crown and even had a peacock feather stuck in it. It was not just a costume. Her face shone with a Divine splendor, and one felt that one was really seeing the Lord Krishna Himself. Chandru pushed me near to her. She affectionately embraced me and passed her hand down my back along my painful spinal column. Her entire body was vibrating at an amazing speed. She then looked me straight in the eyes. Those eyes, where had I seen such eyes? Ratnamji had such eyes in his moments of absorption; Ramana had such eyes always. They were the eyes of a person who is one with the Supreme, full of Peace and dancing as it were with an Inner Bliss. She again affectionately embraced me, and I burst into tears.

If God ever existed on earth, it was in the person of Ammachi. I had at last come to the treasure of treasures. She motioned for me to stand near her. From there, I watched how she attended on each person who came to her. She gave an affectionate embrace to each one and pressed her finger between their eyebrows for a moment. She then gave them a piece of banana and some consecrated water to drink and spoke reassuring words to them. If they had some disease, she touched them on the diseased part. Little children were first allowed to come to her in the temple. They came mainly for the banana! Ammachi's expression of Inner Bliss and unshakable Peace did not change even for a moment. She stood there for five or six hours, until the last person had had Darshan, or audience. There was no hurry. She showed the same patience and concern for men as well as women, for children as well as elderly people, for the rich as well as the poor. This was real equality of mind. She was perfectly conscious and aware of everything that was going on. There was nothing in common with persons whom I had seen that were possessed by Divine Grace. This was a God Realized Soul established in perfect equanimity. What a wonder that she could conceal herself so perfectly that no one could understand who or what she was! I sat there in wonder. In this tiny fishing village was living such a one incognito. I had heard that such people do exist who hide their identity as perfected sages. I was now seeing one for myself. I had come for reasons of health. I now felt ashamed of my selfishness and decided to take refuge in this Great Soul for showing me the way to God-Realization.

With great reluctance I came out of the temple and laydown in the house. Due to pain and weakness, I simply could not sit or stand there any longer, though I wished to stay forever. At the end of Krishna Bhava, Ammachi came into my room along with some other devotees and sat on the floor. I got off my bed and lay on the floor. I felt too humble to lie on a higher level than she was sitting.

"How did you like Krishna?" she asked.

"I think that you are very deceitful pretending that you know nothing, while in fact you know everything," I replied. She laughed.

"Really, I don't know anything," she said, "I am only a crazy girl." Crazy, indeed!

After half an hour, Ammachi reentered the temple. This time she sang a song to Devi, the Divine Mother. Again her body shook, and after a few minutes she stood there as Kali, the fierce aspect of the Divine Mother. Though compassion and grace Itself, the Divine Mother takes a fierce form in order to instill fear into mankind so that they will seriously correct their erring ways.

A good parent must be kind and loving, but at the same

time he should not hesitate to punish or discipline a child who is going in the wrong way. If the child has no sense of fear and reverence for his parents, he will not hesitate to do whatever he likes, good or bad. The ancients never believed, as present-day psychologists do that children should be allowed to grow as they like, like wild weeds. Life has a purpose and a goal, and to achieve that, a keen sense of right and wrong needs to be cultivated in childhood. It is the duty of parents to instill these values into their children. Moral sense is not natural to the human animal but must be taught and acquired.

Ammachi's fierce form, holding a sword in one hand and a trident in the other, inspired the people coming to her for favours to keep their minds pure, at least for the time they were in her presence. Though not concentrating on God even for one minute in the 24 hour day, a worldly devotee could attain intense concentration for a couple of hours while staying near her. With the passage of time, as more and more spiritual aspirants came to her, Ammachi's fierce aspect during Devi Bhava gradually underwent a change, until it became absolutely calm and serene. She even ceased to hold the sword or trident in her hands, holding only flowers instead.

I entered the temple and was asked to sit next to Ammachi. She kept my head on her lap and was stroking my back. I felt that I was really in the lap of the Divine Mother Herself. Her appearance and personality were totally different from that of Krishna or Ammachi. I wondered how these distinct personalities could exist at the same time in one person. She was obviously fully aware of what was going on at all times. The person was the same, but the personality and appearance were changing. I decided to ask her about it afterwards.

I sat there as long as I could and then went and lay down in the house. The darshan finished at 4:00 a.m., at which time she called me to the temple, after changing back to her normal mood. I had brought a small tape recorder with me as suggested by Chandru, so that Ammachi could hear some songs of Swamiji. She asked me to play them. While hearing them, she closed her eyes and tears ran down her cheeks. She was obviously in ecstasy. Was this the same person I had been seeing as God Himself only a few hours ago? I sat with her for awhile longer and then went to lie down, but sleep would not come. There was a strong current of Bliss going through my body, which made sleep impossible. In fact, for the next three days, I got practically no sleep at all.

The next morning, Ammachi came to see how I was. I decided to take the opportunity to clear my doubt.

"Would you tell me what your experience is at the time of the Bhava?" I asked.

"While singing to Krishna or Devi, I see that particular aspect of the Supreme. Offering myself completely to That, I feel myself merge into Him or Her and become completely identified with Them." Saying this, she made a sign like a V with two of her fingers and, bringing them together, showed that the two became one.

"Why do you pretend that you know nothing about what happens during the Bhava? You are obviously fully conscious. I have heard from Chandru that you have suffered much at the hands of your relatives and some ignorant villagers who believe that you are crazy. Couldn't you have told them the truth?" I asked.

"I have undertaken a particular job as entrusted to me by God. I want the people to worship God, not me. They feel that God is coming in me three nights a week, and with that faith, they come here and get their problems solved. Besides, most of these people don't know the ABC's of spiritual life. Even if I were to tell them the truth, who would understand? More than anything, if one sees everything as God, will there be any sense that I am different and the others are different? One who feels that he is something special and that others are floundering in ignorance has certainly a long way to go to realize God."

With great difficulty I learned some of Ammachi's life history. Being naturally humble, she talked about herself only after much coaxing. Even then, she became restless and left before finishing any particular incident.

The seed of devotion was in her heart from her earliest years. She considered Krishna as her all in all and started to compose songs to Him even at the age of five. She always kept a little picture of Him in her petticoat and then took it out and talked to Him. When she was eight or nine, her mother fell sick and the burden of the housework fell on her shoulders. She was forced to stop going to school, although she did go to a parochial school to learn sewing. Her mother and brother were strict disciplinarians and did not hesitate to beat her or kick her if they found anything in her conduct which they felt improper. Her brother especially was a source of great suffering to her, as he was opposed to her devotion to God and abused her for loudly singing the Divine Name.

From 3:00 a.m. until 11:00 at night, she was busy sweeping the yard, feeding the cows, cooking the food, cleaning pots and pans, washing the family's clothes, and doing numerous other jobs. As if this was not enough, she was sent to her relatives' houses to assist in their housework, as well. But all the while, she repeated the Divine Name under her breath, awaiting the day that she might behold her Lord, Sri Krishna. She had the habit of giving away anything in the house to any poor or starving person, which would land her in hot water when she was discovered. Once she was tied to a tree and beaten bloody for having given away her mother's gold bracelet to a starving family.

After reaching her teens, she started to have frequent visions of Lord Krishna and felt herself identified with Him. She would lock herself into the small shrine room in the house and dance and sing in the ecstasy of God-Consciousness, or remain immersed for hours in deep meditation, completely oblivious to her surroundings. Sometimes she was found sitting unconscious in the bathroom, with tears streaming down her face, muttering the words, "Krishna, Krishna." Only with great difficulty could she be aroused to external awareness by her mother. Finally, her internal realization became manifest to the outside world.

While plucking grass for the cows one day, she overheard a discourse about Lord Krishna going on in the neighboring house. Unable to control herself, she ran to the spot and stood there, transfigured as Krishna Himself. The villagers could not make out exactly what had happened to the little girl. Many believed that she was being possessed by Krishna, and others just thought that she was having some kind of fit. None, of course, could understand that she was identified with Him. Crowds started to gather. She was asked to show a miracle in order to prove that she was Krishna. At first she refused, telling them to see the real miracle, God within themselves, but later she agreed to their requests.

A man was asked to bring a small pitcher of water and to dip his finger into it. Lo! the water turned into a kind of sweet jam, which was distributed to all present. From that small pitcher, nearly a thousand villages had their fill of jam, and still the vessel was full. Thenceforth many believed that Krishna had indeed come to bless the village.

This was by no means a blessing for Ammachi. Believing her to be a fraud and a blot on the family name, many villagers and even close relatives tried their best to kill her. They poisoned her food and even took up knives to stab her. However, they failed in all of their attempts and, in fact, met with various disasters shortly after.

About six months passed in this way when one day Ammachi developed a desire to see the Divine Mother, just as she had previously longed for the vision of Krishna. Thinking that through meditation and austerities she could gain the favor of Devi, she spent all of her time immersed in deep meditation on Her form. Sometimes, overwhelmed with restlessness for the vision, she would weep like a child for her mother. She was frequently found lying in the sand, her faced streaked with tears and her hair, ears, and eyes full of mud. She did not think of protecting her body from the elements and sat or lay in the midday sun or heavy rain. Due to the intensity of her longing and her constant thoughts of Devi, she began to perceive the entire universe as Her form. Kissing the trees and embracing the ground, she would weep at the touch of a breeze, feeling it to be full of Mother's Presence. But for all her longing and austerity, she could not behold the personal form of the Divine Mother, which was the object of her longing.

At long last, the Divine Mother appeared before her in a living form and talked with her. She told Ammachi that she had taken birth for the good of the world and should show the people the way to merge into the True Self. Graciously smiling, she then transformed Herself into a brilliant effulgence and merged into Ammachi. In Ammachi's own words, "From that moment onwards, all objective vision ceased, and I came to behold all as my own Self." She came to realize her True Nature as formless and containing all forms, even the form of God, within it. Thenceforth, in addition to Krishna Bhava, Devi Bhava also began. This was by no means the end of Ammachi's troubles.

Perhaps out of feelings of jealousy because huge crowds came to Ammachi, or merely for the fun of making trouble, a number of people continued to harass her. Some informed the police and tried to get her arrested on charges of disturbing the peace, but at the sight of her shining and Blissful countenance, the police bowed down to her and went away. An assassin, hired to do away with her during the darshan time, entered the temple with a knife concealed under his clothes. Mother beamed a benign smile at him, which filled him with remorse at his wicked intention. Falling at her feet, he begged her pardon and became a changed man. At the time of my coming to her, things had more or less calmed down, though there were still a number of villagers opposed to her.

One day, her father having had his fill of troubles brought about by her Divine mood and the consequent crowds, approached her during Devi Bhava and considering Devi as possessing her body, appealed, "I want my daughter back the way she was before you came. Please go away."

"If I go," she replied, "your daughter will become a corpse." Not heeding her words, the father insisted that his demand be met. That moment, Ammachi fell down dead on the spot. For eight hours, there was not a sign of life in her body. An uproar ensued, and the father was blamed for being the cause of her untimely death. Lamps were lit around her dead body, and prayers were offered to God to bring her back to life. Realizing his mistake and repenting bitterly, the father fell flat on the ground in front of the temple and wept, crying out, "Forgive me, O Divine Mother! I am an ignorant man. I will never repeat such words again. Please bring my daughter back to life." Slowly, slight movements became visible in Ammachi's body. At last, her physical condition returned to normal. From that time onwards, her parents ceased to put any restrictions on her, and she was allowed to do more or less as she pleased.

Ammachi had two unmarried sisters, who were looking after the housework and also attending school. Quite a few young men, attracted by Ammachi's motherly affection and spiritual talk, wished to spend more time with her after darshan, but her father would not allow it. He feared that their intentions may not be so innocent and some problems would arise in relation to his other daughters. He chased these boys away as soon as the darshan ended.

Chandru was one such young man and was feeling pained by the father's conduct. One day he appealed to her, "If your father continues to act like this, how will this place ever became an ashram or place of refuge for sincere spiritual aspirants? He is unkind to you and to those who want to stay near you. Besides, there is nobody here to look after your needs. You don't even have a blanket to cover yourself with or proper food to eat. I can't bear to see things going on like this."

Consoling him, Ammachi smiled and told him, "My son, do not worry. You go to Arunachala and take a vow of silence for 41 days. Everything will become all right, after your return. At Arunachala, you will find the people who will look after me and the future ashram. You will also find children coming from countries outside of India who are my own. You will see. The day will come when father will welcome you as his own son with love and affection." Chandru had gone to Arunachala, and we had met shortly thereafter.

It was now the third day of my stay with Ammachi. All day long, I had been smelling a Divine Perfume. I thought that perhaps it was incense being used in the temple but could not find it there. I asked Ammachi where I could get such an incense. She laughed and told me, "Such a scent is not available in any shop. That smell exists within each one, but only yogis know how to bring it out."

I had heard that Ramana had occasionally blessed some of his devotees through the power of his eyes. It was as if beams of subtle light emanated from his eyes and, when he touched someone, that person gained various spiritual experiences. I asked Ammachi if she would or could do the same. "I am a crazy girl. I cannot do anything," she replied, laughing.

That night was darshan. I remained in the temple for as long as I could during both the Bhavas. I felt the atmosphere within the temple charged with spiritual peace. Meditation came with very little effort. I went and lay down behind the temple. I did not feel like going into the house. I wanted to be as near to Ammachi as possible. The darshan was finishing, and Chandru came to call me. He said that Devi was calling me to come to the front of the temple. I came around to the front of the temple and stood facing her. Seeing me there, she walked briskly over to me and gave me an affectionate hug. Then bending down, she whispered into my ear, "My son, do not worry, your body will become better." She then slowly backed up into the temple and was standing in the front door looking at me. As she was looking at me I noticed that her face was getting brighter and brighter. Gradually, that brightness expanded so much that it engulfed her whole body and then the temple and even the surroundings. I could see nothing but that brilliant, but soothing, Light. Suddenly, the effulgence contracted to the size of a pinpoint, its brilliance making me squint. A moment later, it stopped. I was once again seeing Ammachi smiling at me. The temple doors were closed, and the darshan ended.

I clearly felt that Ammachi had entered into me. My mind was full of the thought of her alone and I clearly felt her presence within. I felt that I had gotten a glimpse of her true form, Divine Light. I wondered at her masterly way of concealing her identity as a great sage and making herself appear quite dull and even crazy at times. This was indeed a unique personality.

There were sages who after 40 or 50 years of intense meditation somehow attained Self-Realization, but this was quite a different case. From the age of 16 or 17, she had been established in the Supreme State and had used It in this unique way for the good of the common man, without revealing her identity nor minding the abuses heaped on her. She never lost her patience but showed equal love to all who sought her, even those who sought to harm her.

Talking about the people who had tried to harm her,

she said one day, "It was their misguided conceptions that made them speak and behave the way they did. They could not realize the significance and purpose of spiritual life. That being the case, why should we be angry with them? Look at these beautiful roses. What a fine fragrance. But what do we give them to make them grow? Manure! What a difference between the beautiful flower and the bad-smelling manure. Likewise, impediments are the fertilizer which makes us grow spiritually. To create trouble is the nature of the ignorant. We must pray to God to forgive them and to lead them to the right path."

The next morning Ammachi came to me and asked if I had enjoyed darshan the previous night. I told her of my experience.

"You are very lucky. I felt as if my Inner Light came out of my eyes and merged into you. I wondered if you had felt anything," she said.

Ramana's 100th birthday celebration was due to start in three days. It was to be a very grand function. Although I wanted to stay with Ammachi, I also wanted to attend the function at Arunachala. Knowing my heart, Ammachi told me to go back to Arunachala and see the celebration there. She told Chandru that he should go with me and help me for as long as I needed. She felt that, as he could not remain with her, he should at least have the company of an aspirant on the path. Besides, I needed someone to look after me. I asked her if I could come back and stay permanently with her, as that was my ardent desire.

"If father has no objection you may come and stay," she replied. Approaching her father, I requested him to allow me to stay. He agreed but said that it would be a good idea to construct a hut for myself. That being the only condition, I told him that I would return soon. Ammachi then told me that the influence of some negative force was on me and was partly responsible for my sickness. She said that I should stay in Tiruvannamalai for 41 days and perform a particular rite which would counteract that force. She also explained the details of the rite.

Ammachi called her father and requested him to give us a dancing exhibition. As a young man, he had learned the traditional dance of Kerala—kathakali. He started to dance around the room. He was no longer a young man; he had become bow-legged and had a huge belly like a blimp. Ammachi was rolling on the floor with laughter. The more we laughed, the faster he danced and bounced about like a huge ball. At last he stopped, panting for breath.

As I was taking leave of her, Ammachi removed the rosary of rudraksha beads from around my neck. "I like this," she said. I told her that I would get them strung in silver and bring them to her when I returned. Giving me a motherly hug, she told me, "Don't worry. I am always with you." She then accompanied me to the boat landing and stood there until we had reached the other side of the backwaters.

A taxi was waiting there to take us to Chandru's house about 40 miles away. As soon as I got into the taxi, I burst into tears, recalling the affection that she had shown me. I could not control myself until we had gone four or five miles. Chandru looked at me in wonder. This crying was not a new thing any longer, and so he refrained from asking me what was the matter. An indescribable Bliss was filling my mind, and I could not think of anything except Ammachi. Chandru started to talk about something, but I could not answer him. My mind simply refused to think. Though still sick and weak, I no longer cared much about my body. She had said that I would become better. It must be so, I thought.

After reaching Chandru's house, I felt hungry for the first time in months. I requested his mother to prepare some rice and vegetables, which I ate without experiencing any stomach pain. From that day onwards, I was able to eat normal food. Because of this, I slowly gained in strength, so that I could move about and even do small jobs. Although the weakness and pains in the back persisted, they were not as they had been when I had gone to Ammachi.

The next day, we boarded the train for Tiruvannamalai. After going along for about half an hour, I started to smell the Divine fragrance that I had smelled in Ammachi's presence. I searched my bags and found that the fragrance was emanating from the rosary she had touched. It was so strong that it was if someone had poured perfume over it. I put it in a plastic bag and packed it away. After a few minutes, I noticed the same fragrance again. I started to feel as if I would weep. Suddenly the odor changed to that of jasmine flowers, then to fresh lemons, ordinary incense, and finally to cooked tapioca root, all things which one could find near Ammachi. At the time that we had seen her, she was eating tapioca root instead of rice as a staple food.

I called Chandru and asked him if he could smell any of those things. He could not. I asked him to keep his nose next to mine and see if he could smell anything. The co-passengers must have been wondering what we were up to. Still he could not smell anything, although the odors were filling my nostrils as if the things were being held right up to my nose. It must be Ammachi's play, I thought. Chandru sat down in his seat. After two minutes he exclaimed, "Now I smell it! Now I smell it!" During the 16-hour journey, the odors made themselves known off and on, along with a feeling of Ammachi's presence. No doubt this is an abstract idea, that someone could be present though not visible. This was, however, our impression, and it was later confirmed as correct by Ammachi herself.

For the next 41 days, we remained in Tiruvannamalai. The centenary celebration of Ramana's birth was indeed grand and done on an impressive scale. I was glad that I could witness it, but although I was standing before the tomb of Ramana, my mind was with Ammachi. I felt like one who, though holding on to a tree, was being swept away by a tornado. For 11 years, the center and support of my life had been Ramana. Even my association with Ratnamji and Swamiji had seemed to be provided and guided by Ramana. From this tomb, I felt a living presence which had been a source of succor and solace to my often-confused mind. In fact, even the subtle light or current of awareness which was making itself felt within my mind had been somehow equated with Ramana's presence.

Now, even though standing before him, I felt that inner presence to be Ammachi. Was this the effect of her having entered into me on the night before my departure from her? I had no doubt that it was, and I was not sorry about it. The company and guidance of a Realized Soul who is living in the body is at any time preferable to that of one who has left his physical sheath. I consoled myself by thinking that Father had decided to send me to Mother after having reared me to some extent.

The rite which Ammachi had advised me to do involved going in front of any temple before 2:00 a.m. and, while praying to God to remove the influence which was affecting me, pass a lit firebrand over and around my head. This I did for the entire 41 days. During this time, Chandru was doing his best to attend to my needs. It was a trying time for him. Ratnamji had trained me in such a strict fashion that every action had to be done in a particular way. Even a matchbox should not be placed haphazardly. I insisted that Chandru do the same. He, of course, had to struggle those 41 days but later admitted that it stood him in good stead when he had to leave Ammachi for the next four years to study Vedanta in Bombay.

It was at this time that I met Gayatri. She was from Australia and had come to Arunachala without any prior plan. Circumstances had somehow brought her, and she had been living there for the past year or so, cooking for some of the local devotees and leading a very austere life. She had absolutely no money and, on some days, even had to pluck leaves off the trees so that she would have something to feed others and herself. In some mysterious way, a little money or food would come to her now and then, and she was able to continue on like this. She had heard about Ammachi from Chandru in the course of a conversation and had an intense desire to see her. She actually wished that she could become close enough to Ammachi to be able to serve her as a personal attendant.

Gayatri had an exceptionally innocent mind and she could harbor no ill will towards any one, for any length of time, however much they might abuse her. In addition to that, she did not want to lead a worldly life and was depending on God to provide for her and show her the way to realize Him. One day while meditating, she saw a flash of light and saw Ammachi as a living form within herself. A cry of "Mother, Mother, Mother," spontaneously arose within her, and then everything subsided into a profound stillness. Thenceforth, she became extremely restless to go to Ammachi. When she heard that we would be leaving shortly to go back to Ammachi, she requested us to take her. Chandru looked at me and said, "I think this girl may become Ammachi's attendant. Let us take her with us." After making arrangements for someone to look after the houses in Tiruvannamalai, the three of us departed. Little did we know that an entirely new life was about to open up before us.

"Mother has gone for her bath. She will be coming back soon." It was one of the boys who used to visit Ammachi on days when there was no darshan. He had been sitting in front of the temple meditating. We sat waiting for Mother. Within a few minutes, she came running like a little girl and laughingly greeted us. We bowed down at her feet and introduced Gayatri to her. She scrutinized Gayatri and then sat with us. Chandru told her about our experience in the train.

"When you left from this place, you were very sick," she said looking at me. "I was thinking of you, and that is why you felt my presence."

"Mother, is it enough for you just to think of a person and they will feel as if you are there? How is it possible?" I asked her.

"Son, concentration is needed and only then is it possible. I first think, 'So and so is staying in a certain place. But that place and all places are within me.' Thinking thusly, my mind goes to that person. If his mind is a bit pure he will certainly feel something. If you ask me why I should go to any particular person, I cannot say. It strikes me like that, that is all." Saying this, she began to laugh. Some small children were playing nearby. She got up and started to run after them, playing tag. She was running and screaming just like them. Except for her size, one would have thought she was about six or seven years old. After about 15 minutes, she returned to us, out of breath.

"One should spend some time every day with small children," she said. "Their innocence will rub off on us, and we will enjoy the happiness of a child. Actually, our True Nature is to be an innocent child of God, but we let it get covered over by things like lust, anger, and greed. The same innocence that you see in the eyes of a child can be seen in the eyes of a God-Realized person."

Mother, as that is how we addressed her, asked Gayatri to sit next to her and meditate. After a few minutes she pressed her finger between Gayatri's eyebrows and watched her intensely. She seemed to have a definite purpose in doing so. After holding her finger like that for a few minutes, she suddenly smiled. Whatever it was that she had wanted to do, she apparently had done it. Gayatri slowly opened her eyes. She was very shy and hesitant before Mother.

"Don't be so shy, daughter. If a girl wants to go up in spiritual life, that shyness should go. Some of the qualities of a man, like detachment and courage, should be assimilated by a woman if she is to succeed. Ladies are not generally interested in renouncing worldly life to attain God. Who would keep the creation going? But if their interest is somehow kindled, then they can make even faster progress than men."

It was decided that I should be accommodated in the house, Mother and Gayatri would sleep inside the temple, and Chandru would rest wherever he could find a place out of the cold and rain. That night Mother made Gayatri sleep by her side and fell asleep with her legs on Gayatri's. Mother's childlike innocence coupled with her motherly affection and advise touched Gayatri's heart and bound her immediately to her. By the second day, she had decided never to return to Arunachala. In those days, except when she was in meditation, Mother spent all of her time with us, feeding us with her own hands, joking with us, or singing songs and telling interesting anecdotes. There was never a dull moment, and we found that, as the days went by, Mother alone existed in our thoughts.

Darshan started at 6:00 p.m. and continued until 6:00 or 7:00 a.m. Even after that, Mother would sit in front of the temple talking to visiting devotees until 10:00 or 11:00 a.m. We could not understand how she could bear such a strain day after day. We had no inclination to sleep on those three nights. When Mother was staying awake all night to help the people, how could we comfortably sleep? At first, the local people could not understand why two foreigners wanted to stay in a tiny fishing village with a "crazy" girl like Ammachi, but they soon came to look upon us as some of their own who simply felt a powerful attraction, as they themselves did, towards Mother. Mother prohibited us from revealing her true identity to the visitors or villagers. She felt that their faith should not be disturbed, as they were getting their problems resolved through such faith.

"All will come at the right time, children. Who brought you here? The same One will bring about whatever is necessary, when it is necessary. Let us just do our duty without having any desire for the fruits. Mother needs no propaganda. Those who have purity of heart and thirst for God will come and seek and understand Her." She continued playing the double role of God during darshan time and a somewhat crazy, but charming, girl at other times.

Shortly after our coming to Mother to settle near her permanently, a hut was constructed which was to become the first ashram building. It was a single room, big enough so that half of it could be used as a kitchen and half as a place to live and sleep. Mother and Gayatri stayed on one side and Balu, one of the young men who was lucky enough to get the father's permission to stay with us, and I stayed on the other side. The cooking was done by Gayatri. Though constructed of coconut leaves, it was enough to protect us from the elements. Unfortunately, because it was the only shelter available, as many visitors as could squeeze into it would occupy it on darshan nights, leaving hardly any room for us to lie down.

Most of our time was spent in trying to adjust to the constant flow of people coming in and out of the hut at all hours of the day and night. It became a full time job to keep people from disturbing Mother, after She had finally gone to sleep. They came whenever they could find time, and they never considered that she may not have slept for two or three days. Many times I had to lie in the doorway so that no one could get in, thus allowing Mother to get a few hours rest. To see her rest undisturbed became my greatest joy. The world is all praise for a person who manifests a little selflessness once in a while. Mother was the very embodiment of selflessness. She was ready to give over her life just to relieve the most common man of his sufferings. To do that, she gave up sleep, food, and anything that could be called her own. One example may suffice to make the point clear.

One night, the darshan finished a bit early, around

4:00 a.m. It was the rainy season, so the crowds were not as large as at other times. After darshan, Mother sat on the temple veranda until nearly 5:00 or 5:30 talking with some devotees. After much coaxing by us, she finally agreed to come into the hut and rest. We had just lain down and turned off the lights when we heard a voice at the door. It was a lady who had missed the bus to come to this place. She had walked quite a distance all night long in order to reach here and see Mother during Darshan time. Seeing that the darshan was over, she thought that at least she could see Ammachi before going back. We were not inclined to open the door.

"Open the door," Mother insisted. "I'm not here to enjoy rest and comfort. If I can alleviate the people's sufferings even a bit, that is enough for me. Their happiness is my happiness. Do you realize with what great difficulty this woman has come here just to unburden her heart to me? Some of the people coming here are so poor they must save their pennies for days to pay for their bus journey. Before you all came here, I was free to meet whoever came, whenever they came. In the future also, I must be allowed to do so or I will sleep outside as I was doing before. Do I need this blanket or this pillow? I had nothing before, and even now I need nothing. Only to please you am I using these things." She got up and talked with the lady and, only after comforting her, went to sleep.

Mother, having bound me to her through her affectionate conduct, started to instruct me slowly and subtly. She never gave me any long explanations, but just said a few words or suggested a small change in my way of thinking and doing. Only three or four days after my arrival, she noticed that the temple had not been cleaned, even though it was 7 in the morning. She called me. Still very weak and painful in body, I was spending most of my time lying down. Being herself utterly detached from her body and wanting me also to come up to her level, though that was quite impossible, she told me to clean the temple, and she started to perform this task. I struggled and suffered, but somehow I got through the work. She always seemed to be able to find some work that only I could do. It was not that I did not want to work. Physical labor meant pain, and I wanted to avoid that. Though knowing this was an obstacle to spiritual progress, I still hesitated to inure the pain.

It is said that, just as there are three types of doctors, so also there are three types of Gurus. The first doctor advises the patient and goes away, not even caring to know whether the patient has taken the medicine. This is like a Guru who advises his disciples but does not care to see whether they are acting on his advice and improving. The second type of doctor prescribes the drug and coaxes the patient to take it. This is like a Guru who, being more sincere, shows great patience with a disciple and takes endless pains to explain and coax the disciple to act on the advice given. The last, and best, type of doctor does not hesitate to step on the patient's chest and force the medicine down his throat, knowing that he will not take it otherwise. Ammachi was like the last doctor. Knowing that I would not cast off attachments to the body on my own, she made it compulsory for me to do so. Even during darshan, when I was about to get up, she told me to sit down and found some reason why I should stay there.

"I am Shakti (Power) Herself," She would say. "Won't I give you enough strength to sit here? Worrying about how you are going to feel tomorrow, you want to get up and go away today." Though restless and suffering with pain and weakness, I was surprised to find that I could sit in the temple next to her until the end of the darshan. In fact, on those days I would have my best meditation.

One day, during the rainy season, I caught a slight cold and fever. After the fever subsided, a cough started. This cough became so severe and persistent that I thought I might have contracted some disease of the lungs. It continued for nearly a month. At night I would sit outside, away from the hut, and cough for hours, trying not to disturb the sleep of Mother and the others. I finally went to a doctor who gave me some medicine and told me to take it for one week.

On returning to the ashram, I put the medicine in Mother's hands and asked her to bless it. This was the usual custom of people who wanted to take medicine but also had faith that, by Ammachi's Grace, they would get better without fail. She closed her eyes for a few moments and returned the medicine to me. She had made a resolve, or "sankalpa" as it is called, by the power of which one could be sure of being cured. It is believed that the will power of the Enlightened is perfect and can achieve even the apparently impossible. If they make a serious resolve, its fulfillment is certain whatever the obstacles may be. I took the medicine for a day or two but did not feel any improvement. I had severe pain in the chest while breathing, and I became restless to somehow get relief. I decided to go to another doctor and returned with more medicine. Again I put the medicine in Ammachi's hands, and she again closed her eyes and returned it to me. I tried it for a few days but did not feel any relief. Was there something wrong with her power of resolve? That day she went to a nearby village to pay a visit to some devotee who had invited her there. Feeling that I may become a burden to others, I decided to admit myself into a private hospital and stay there until I was better. I knew that Ammachi, motherly as she was, would not agree to letting me go and stay in a hospital. I therefore took this opportunity, when she was away, and went with her father to a hospital about 10 miles distant.

I stayed there three days, but there was no improvement in sight. Plenty of antibiotics were given, but to no avail. In the meantime, Mother had come to know of my escape but did not say anything. On the third night of my stay I started to feel her presence intensely and, weeping uncontrollably, became restless to go to her. But how was that possible? I had decided not to leave the hospital unless cured. The next morning the doctor came in and gave me some tablets, saying that perhaps I was suffering from some kind of an allergy and not an infection. Just at that moment, Ammachi walked in with about 15 people.

"Son, last night I started to think about you intensely. I felt much for your sufferings and wrote this song to the Divine Mother."

ISWARI JAGAD ISWARI

O Goddess, Goddess of the Universe
O Preserver, O Giver of Grace

O Thou, the Giver of Eternal Salvation
Please rid me of all my sorrows.

I have seen the pleasures of this worldly life
Which is full of afflictions.
Please do not make me suffer
Like the moth that flies into the fire.

Bound by the noose of desire in front,
And the noose of death at the back
O Mother, is it not a pity
To play tying them together?

Showing not the wrong path
O Eternal One, shed Thy Grace on me
O Mother, who are the Destroyer of misery,
Please remove the burden of sorrows.

What is seen today is not there tomorrow;
O Pure Consciousness, Everything is your play.
Whatever "is" has no destruction
Anything destructible is ephemeral.

O Mother of the Universe,
With joined hands I pray,
To achieve the goal of human birth
O Goddess of the Universe, O Thou in all form
I bow to Your Feet.

"I decided that today I must come here and fetch you. You must come back to the ashram. Do not worry. You will get better soon," she said.

I asked her, "Mother, why did the medicines which you blessed not work?"

"When I made the resolve I thought, 'Let him get better by taking this medicine,' but you would not take it for more than a day or two. Should you not be more patient and give the resolve a chance to work? Like a restless child, you ran from one doctor to another. Even if I bless the medicine, you must take it to make it fruitful," she said.

The doctor of course agreed to let me go, and we returned to the ashram. That night was darshan. The cough was still severe. During Krishna Bhava, I went up to Mother. She put one of her hands on my head and the other on my heart and stood like that, smiling at me for a few moments. She then motioned me to sit down in a corner of the temple. When I sat and looked around, I found to my amazement that a Divine Light was clearly discernible in the face of everyone I looked at. Also, my body felt as if made of wood—not heavy, but insensitive. Though coughing, I did not care at all about it. I enjoyed an intense detachment from my physical frame and a Blissful Intoxication within my mind.

I got up and went out of the temple. Our dinner was served at a fixed time, and I wandered into the kitchen, but I could not make myself eat anything. The food looked and tasted like rubber. Who wanted food at that time? Who could even think of it? I again went into the temple and stayed there for another hour. After about three hours like this, I slowly returned to my usual state. Within two days, the cough began to subside and soon disappeared completely.

Chapter VII

WITH THE DIVINE MOTHER

Ammachi is the Mother of all who came to her, be they men or women, old or young. She looks upon all as her own children; this, in turn, inspired them to look upon her as their own Mother. This brought about a great revolution in the minds of many of the people who sought her presence. They saw that she wanted nothing from anyone, but instead offered her time, food, health, and even rest to them without limit, regardless of who or what they might be. They felt that such a selfless love did not exist anywhere else on this earth. One's own mother might get angry if disobeyed or slighted, but Ammachi even forgave those who tried to kill her and loved them as if they were merely naughty children. She never asked anything of anyone and accepted everyone as they were, dirty, clean, or otherwise.

This Desireless Love bound many people to Mother in a steadfast tie of attachment. Many found that, except in her company, they could find no meaning in their lives. She is ever present in their thoughts. They began to feel that they must rid themselves of their vices, as these were unbefitting a child of hers, even though she never told them so herself. Some of them, even in spite of her protests that she could not support or feed anyone, came to settle near her, leaving their homes, jobs, or schools. The people who decided to remain near her, no matter what she or others might say, were mostly young men who had college degrees but found that the worldly life held no prospect of real happiness in the light of her wonderful, pure, and selfless Love.

While talking to these boys, she emphasized the illusion of seeking happiness through a worldly life; how for the sake of a few moments of pleasure one pays with years of pain. One becomes restless due to the desire for pleasures and, even after enjoying them, the cravings spring up again and again. Repeated enjoyment, far from leading to satisfaction, leads one to boredom and finally despair. If real and lasting happiness does not lie in the endless enjoyment of sensual pleasures, where then does it lie?

Ammachi pointed out to these young men that the same energy used for worldly purposes could be directed to yield the experience of Inner Bliss and Divine Knowledge. Worldly enjoyment saps one's energy and is a slow death, whereas spiritual experience fills one with energy and takes one to realms of Realization and refined Bliss which are unknown to the common man. She would say, "Nectar is deposited at the top of the head in the mystic thousand-petaled lotus, but man never cares to look there, busy as he is with the five senses below." Having herself realized the Truth, her words carried authority which no amount of book learning could give. She lived what she preached. She did not, however, press anyone to take up any spiritual practice, but only exposed them to these ideas.

Two years after my arrival, a group of five or six young men came to settle near Mother. There was no shelter for anyone, so they slept out in the open, under a tree, or on the veranda of the temple. They took no notice of their food or clothing but simply got along with whatever was forthcoming. Mother told them repeatedly that she could not support them, but still they were unwilling to leave her. Her company and her words were all they wanted. One had to admire their spirit of renunciation. Though not burning with the desire for Self-Realization, they nevertheless felt that the worldly life was not the solution to the problems of the search for happiness. They were indifferent to all worldly pleasures and found that Mother's company was their only source of peace and happiness.

Apart from closing their eyes for a few minutes or singing devotional songs during the darshan, one could not however, say that they were on the spiritual path. Though aware of their background and their relation with Ammachi, their lack of seriousness in doing spiritual practice started to irritate me. Their attitude toward Mother was that of children with their mother. The child does not want to do anything except be with the mother. Why strive to become like her? The happiness of her company was enough.

Having sought Ammachi's company for the purpose of going higher in spiritual life and looking upon her as my Guru and Guide, I felt pained when some of the boys did not show her the proper respect due to a Realized Soul. She told me again and again that they did not look upon her the same way I did, and therefore, I should not expect them to act as I did. Their utter lack of discipline started to get on my nerves, and I actually wondered why I was staying on. The company of a saint is no doubt the greatest aid there is for spiritual progress, but the surrounding atmosphere should also be conducive.

Wishing for and expecting an ashram atmosphere around Ammachi and not finding it, I felt that the blame lay on those who had settled there. I started to see their faults and lack of spirituality instead of their good qualities and their detachment from worldly life. My mind became very restless, and I thought of going back to Arunachala. Perhaps I had made the wrong choice by coming here to settle forever. I did not expect things to take such a turn. I had hoped that Mother would come to be known and respected as an Enlightened One and an ashram would form around her. I was disappointed. Such were my thoughts at the time.

When I had all but decided to leave the place, I had a dream one night. I saw Ammachi looking at me with the full moon shining in the sky to her left and the sun shining to her right. She pointed at the sun and said, "Do you see the bright ray of the sun? Like that ray, try to see the ray of Divine Light in each one's eyes." I woke up feeling quite happy. I asked Mother about it the next morning.

"Yes," she said. "You must try to see that Light in each one. If you do not overlook the faults of others, how will you be able to see that innocent Light? You must try to see that innocence in each one." I found this to be very befitting advice. In fact, if one could perfect it, where would be the scope for lust, anger, jealousy, or dislike? She could clearly see the Divine Light in all and so could advise others to do so. Was not her whole life an expression of that experience? She also added that even though one must at first imagine seeing God in everyone, like a rehearsal before the actual performance, later it would become a direct experience. Following her advice, I found my aversion for the visitors and residents dissolving and I reached a new level of inner peace, less and less affected by external circumstances. I still desired that Mother be shown due respect, but this was not to be for some years to come. I had to bypass all my good ideas and high hopes and go deeper into the subtle presence of Ammachi within, not caring for anything but that.

The coming days found more people arriving and settling near Mother. She did not insist that they meditate or have any type of daily routine. The reason was obvious. The people coming to her were not seeking her company out of any desire for spiritual realization, but only for the happiness and peace which they enjoyed in her presence. If she insisted on any sort of discipline, they would run back to their homes and worldly activities. She was in the process of binding them to her through her selfless Love. At the right time, she would start to mold them spiritually.

This is the way of a true Guru. It is not his philosophy or ideals that will keep the relationship between himself and his disciples intact during the ensuing strenuous and prolonged course of spiritual practice, but only the disciple's knowledge that the Guru has infinite and unlimited love and concern for him. A true Guru, after binding his disciple to him through love, will gradually take the disciple through a course of discipline to slowly reveal all the workings of the mind, both gross and subtle, down to the subtlest point of where the very existence of the mind starts. Reaching the "bottom" of the mind, the disciple comes to see the Truth shining within as his Real Self, and finds that the body and mind are unreal projections of that Self, his True Nature. This process is a prolonged one for most aspirants and may even take more than one lifetime. There are many trials and tribulations along the path of Self-Knowledge and renunciation of the false mind. Love is the prime mover of the universe, and only Love can keep one going until the end, in spite of difficulties encountered along the way. If love is lacking from the beginning, the disciple will flee when the going gets a little rough. It is, therefore, the duty of the Guru to instill that sense of love and trust in the heart of the disciple at the beginning of the relationship, overlooking everything else.

This influx of various types of people created a new situation for me which I had never encountered before. I found that I could not open my mouth without someone getting angry at me. Somehow, whatever I said seemed to irritate the people staying near Mother. Unless I kept completely quiet and coalesced in the wishes of others, I had to be ready to be the object of people's dislike and anger. Whatever I said or did was the result of my previous training and discipline, and whatever people coming there were doing was the result of their lack of such discipline and training. Nobody was to blame.

I found that this situation was a unique opportunity for me to cultivate patience and see God in all. Whatever others might say or do, I had to maintain a pure and calm mind and not be affected by the circumstances. Had Ammachi not done the same for so many years? I felt that this was her way making me walk in the path she had trod in order to become like her. It would not be enough to know about her trials and sufferings and resultant victories. I had to experience them myself. Then only would that information become practical. To make clear exactly what I refer to, I will narrate two incidents to demonstrate this point.

One day I was having a severe migraine headache. I was already weak, and the severity of the pain completely incapacitated me. I could not even walk without holding a wall for support. I had taken a powerful drug to lessen the pain, but this had the effect of increasing the weakness and causing thirst. In that state, I asked one of the residents for a glass of water to drink. He looked at me as if I had asked for a seven-course meal and walked away. I waited for about half an hour, but no water was forthcoming. I then crawled and somehow got it myself. Unfortunately, my hand was shaking and I spilled some of the water on the floor. At that time, another of the residents came into the hut. I asked him for a cloth to wipe up the water. He went out and came back with a dirty cloth, and threw it in my face with a look of irritation. I felt a bit pained at heart and went and lay down behind the temple. Ammachi came over to me and asked me what was the matter. I told her what had happened. She said, "You must look upon them as children. Whatever a child may do, one should not feel angry or hurt, knowing that they are ignorant." She then kept quiet and silently sat with me for some time.

On another occasion, I purchased some pancakes for Mother, thinking that she might eat them in the morning after the darshan was over. The shop was open only at night, I got them and put them in a container. I felt very sleepy, however, so I asked one of the people who would be awake at that hour to give them to Mother when she came.

"Mother will not eat what you have brought. Don't you know that she doesn't like pancakes? If you want, you can give them to her yourself." I had seen her eat pancakes a number of times and knew that what was said was untrue. I muttered the Name of God to myself and kept quiet.

It soon became second nature not to mind the way I was treated by others. In fact, I even started to take a kind of delight in being abused. I would note clearly whether or not my mind was affected by the words and try to remain as a witness within, unchanging and calm. Ratnamji had once told me, "As a devotee, others may praise you and put you on a pedestal. You may think that you are unaffected by their praise and even say that it is God in their form who is praising. But you will know if you are really unaffected by praises only when you receive the opposite, blame. One who is unaffected by abuse is also indifferent to praise. If one cares not for pain, pleasure also cannot hold one bound. One should always test oneself and be sure that one is not fooling oneself thinking that pleasant things do not affect one. Only if you are indifferent to the painful side of life and take it as God's or Guru's Sweet will, will you not be sidetracked by the pleasant side of things."

Forbearance in the face of pain, physical or mental, is an essential quality for attaining abidance in the Self, where even great pain or sorrow leaves Inner Bliss untouched. I felt that, in order to help me reach that state, Ammachi was giving me many opportunities for practice. In fact, I became convinced of it soon afterward, due to a peculiar incident.

One day Mother was invited to visit a devotee's house about 10 miles away. There was to be devotional singing for about two hours in the night. At that time, there were four people who could play the harmonium (a hand-pumped organ), which was essential for the musical accompaniment. One of these four was a boy who had gone on an errand and had not yet returned. I was another. I had suffered all day with a severe headache, and I could hardly sit up. Mother called me to come with her.

"Mother, my head is about to break," I complained. "Cannot someone else go along and play the harmonium?" "What!" she exclaimed. "How is that possible? If you don't come it will not be all right. You must come."

I had decided to surrender to my Guru, come what may. Now was my chance to put this into practice. I accompanied her to the house and sat down to play. Tears flowed from my eyes, not because I felt sorrow, but because of the pressure and pain in my head. I was forced to detach my mind from my body and played without caring for the consequences. I thought, at that time, that this is what death must be like. One must simply bear the pain of it, being unable to do anything else. Afterwards, when food was served, I could not eat due to a nauseous sensation in my stomach. After returning home, I finally fell asleep. The next day, as Ammachi walked by me, she mentioned to someone standing next to me, "See how cruel I am! Even though he had such a painful headache, I made him play the harmonium." In fact, this was what she felt was effective to make me reach higher planes of spirituality.

This should not lead one to believe that Ammachi is cruel to her children. If anything, she is just the opposite, but she will not hesitate to do what she knows to be for her disciples' spiritual good, pleasant or painful.

On another occasion, when I had a similar headache, Mother called me and started to talk about something. I told her that it was impossible for me to concentrate on what she was saying due to the severity of the pain. She told me to go and lie down. I went to my room, and she went for the evening devotional singing in front of the temple. She stopped singing in the middle of the second song. Just at that moment, a soothing light appeared in my mental field, and then it disappeared. After a few moments, it reappeared and sucked all the pain into itself, as it were. It then disappeared and Mother started to sing again. Feeling quite all right, I got up, and went to the temple, and sat there to hear the rest of the singing.

There were other occasions when Mother relieved me of excessive pain. During Krishna Bhava one day, I entered the temple and stood in a corner looking at her. I was having unusually intense body pains. I entered the temple with the idea to meditate. She turned and looked at me with a steady gaze, and I felt the pain drawn out of my body. I found that in her presence my meditation became deep very quickly, flowing like a current of water. What might not be achieved in many years of solitary meditation was easily done in Mother's Divine Presence.

As the days passed, I slowly came to realize what a great master Ammachi was. However many people came to her, she understood their spiritual levels, their problems, their mental make up, and how to raise them spiritually and, if necessary, materially. She knew exactly how to act at any moment, with any number of people. Her actions did not seem to require any thought, but rather flowed from a spontaneous source always befitting the situation. What is medicine for one may be poison for another, and this principle was fully known to her. In fact, something which was medicine for someone at one time might harm the same person at another time.

In my own relationship with her, I found a gradual but definite change. When I first came to her, she showered her motherly affection on me. She even fed me with her own hands. She spent most of her time with me and one or two others who were living there. Feeling restless when I could not be near her even for a few moments, I told her so. "You will soon feel me within you always and not care about the external presence," she reassured me. Her words turned out to be prophetic.

Going deeper within day after day, as a result of her instructions and the peculiar situations in which I found myself, I started to feel her subtle presence clearly within my mind. I preferred to be alone, contemplating on that, rather than sitting in her presence. Of course, at the time of Dar- . shan, I felt a particularly intense degree of concentration which I made good use of. But, as I was going deeper, I noticed a particular change in Mother's attitude towards me. Whenever I came near, she ignored me. Even when I was talking to her, she would abruptly get up and walk away. I could not at first understand this change in her attitude towards me. Then an incident took place which opened my eyes.

Even though I had been meditating for many years, the Bliss of Union with God still seemed to be far away. I knew that a Realized Soul had the power to remove the screen of ignorance covering the Reality in a disciple's mind. I had asked Ammachi about it, and she had admitted that it could be done, but only if the disciple was perfectly ripe for it. He should have purified himself through spiritual practice to such an extent that he had become like a ripe fruit about to fall off the tree. I decided to ask Mother why she would not bless me with such grace, since I had been trying for such a long time. I did not, of course, realize that my question implied a certain amount of false pride that I had reached a perfectly ripe state. I approached her when she was alone.

"Mother, you have said that the Enlightened have the power to liberate their disciples. Won't you do the same for me?" I asked. "I have also heard of many instances where the Guru has blessed the disciple with the Supreme State." I proceeded to narrate stories of great saints who had gained the highest Realization by the Grace of their Guru.

"They had supreme devotion for their Guru," she began. "When a disciple has such self-effacing devotion for his Master, then even without asking, the thought arises in the mind of the Guru to bless the disciple with the complete removal of ignorance and the resultant Liberated State. Until then, if one has not reached that degree of maturity, even if one lies down in front of me and commits suicide, saying that I must bless him with Realization, I cannot and will not. The moment you are ready for it, it will flash in my mind to do so, and not before then."

"Then what am I to do until then?" I asked. "Shall I just wait?"

"If you simply wait, you will have to wait a long time indeed! Do not wait, work!" she said emphatically.

"Can you not suggest something that I can do which will bless me with that grace?" I persisted.

Mother kept silent. I waited nearly five minutes and asked her again the same question. Still she kept quiet. What was she to say? She had already answered me, and there remained nothing else to be said. She finally got up and went away.

A few days later, I again approached her with the same request. Again, I was met with silence. I gradually came to understand that her silence meant that I should be silent. In fact, the very uprising of the question meant that my surrender and faith in her were not full and, if such were the case, where was complete ripeness and maturity? If I could make my mind utterly desireless, I would come to realize through direct experience that my innermost Self, concealed under the cloud of various subtle and gross desires, was exactly the thing which I was seeking. By asking Mother to reveal the Truth to me, I was thickening the veil and putting the Realization further off. To keep my mind on the Mother within and prevent all other thoughts from arising seemed to be the essence of all spiritual practice. I decided to pursue it wholeheartedly thenceforth. In spite of my resolve, however, I did ask Mother a few more times about some unnecessary doubts, in answer to which she kept silent. Her silence was an indication to me that I must control my mind and make it perfectly silent. There was no other way.

Because a foreign national cannot live in India more than six months unless he is attached to an institution for purposes of study or business, it became necessary to have the ashram officially registered with the government. Following this, Ammachi felt that the devotees residing there should begin to follow some sort of discipline. To that end, she drew up a compulsory timetable to be followed by those who chose to live near her. Her whole attitude began to change at this stage from that of a mother to that of a spiritual guide. Though the same motherly concern and patience was there, she started to wholeheartedly advise her devotees to follow this or that course of spiritual practice. In fact, she even went so far as to say that those who did not want to do meditation and other spiritual practices could go home by the next bus. This was a bit of a shock to those who had been living a carefree life, thinking that it would be like that forever.

For me, it was a great relief and even somewhat of a surprise to see Mother taking the reins into her hands to make her children into saints. I started to feel more at home, and the atmosphere started to change from that of a big house to that of an ashram, full of spiritual aspirants engaged in an austere and dedicated life. Mother asked me to look after the discipline of the residents in a general way, as it was not possible for her to be with everyone all the time. I was to report to her any trespass in the daily routine.

While the life in the ashram was undergoing vast changes, things outside of the ashram were also changing. More and more people started to recognize Ammachi as a living saint who had realized the Supreme. Her unique universal Love, patience, and concern for all became known. She was invited to all of the important temples in Kerala and was received with all honors. Also the type of people visiting the ashram changed more to those who wanted spiritual betterment. Things had, at last, become as I had wished for long ago. Enjoying inner peace, I recalled the words of Mother as sung by her in a song describing the purpose of her life:

Dancing in the Path of Bliss,
Likes and dislikes disappeared. . . .
And forgetting myself, I merged in
The Divine Mother renouncing all enjoyments.

Countless are the yogis who,
born in India, have followed
The great principles of Divine wisdom
as revealed by the Ancients.
Numerous are the naked truths
expressed by them
That can save mankind from misery.

The Divine Mother told me to inspire the people
With the desire for Liberation. Therefore,
I proclaim to the whole world the
Sublime Truth that She uttered:

"Oh Man, merge in your Self.
Oh Man, merge in your Self."

For those interested in learning more about the teachings of
Mata Amritanandamayi please contact:

```
        Mata Amritanandamayi Center
               P.O. Box 613
        San Ramon, CA.  94583-0613
             ph: (510) 537-9417
```